Egypt

Also from Westphalia Press
westphaliapress.org

Egypt

La Mort de Philae

by Pierre Loti

Translated by W. P. Baines

WESTPHALIA PRESS
An imprint of Policy Studies Organization

Egypt: La Mort de Philae
All Rights Reserved © 2015 by Policy Studies Organization

Westphalia Press
An imprint of Policy Studies Organization
1527 New Hampshire Ave., NW
Washington, D.C. 20036
info@ipsonet.org

ISBN-13: 978-1-63391-172-7
ISBN-10: 1633911721

Cover design by Taillefer Long at Illuminated Stories:
www.illuminatedstories.com

Daniel Gutierrez-Sandoval, Executive Director
PSO and Westphalia Press

Rahima Schwenkbeck, Director of Media and Marketing
PSO and Westphalia Press

Updated material and comments on this edition
can be found at the Westphalia Press website:
www.westphaliapress.org

EGYPT

EGYPT

(LA MORT DE PHILÆ)

BY

PIERRE LOTI

TRANSLATED FROM THE FRENCH BY

W. P. BAINES

CONTENTS

vi   # Contents

A WINTER MIDNIGHT BEFORE
THE GREAT SPHINX

CHAPTER I

A NIGHT wondrously clear and of a colour
unknown to our climate; a place of dreamlike
aspect, fraught with mystery. The moon of a
bright silver, which dazzles by its shining,
illumines a world which surely is no longer
ours; for it resembles in nothing what may be
seen in other lands. A world in which everything is suffused with rosy colour beneath the
stars of midnight, and where granite symbols
rise up, ghostlike and motionless.

Is that a hill of sand that rises yonder? One
can scarcely tell, for it has as it were no shape,
no outline; rather it seems like a great rosy
cloud, or some huge, trembling billow, which
once perhaps raised itself there, forthwith to
become motionless for ever. . . . And from
out this kind of mummified wave a colossal
human effigy emerges, rose-coloured too, a nameless, elusive rose; emerges, and stares with fixed
eyes and smiles. It is so huge it seems unreal,
as if it were a reflection cast by some mirror
hidden in the moon. . . . And behind this mon-

3

ster face, far away in the rear, on the top of
those undefined and gently undulating sandhills, three apocalyptic signs rise up against the
sky, three rose-coloured triangles, regular as the
figures of geometry, but so vast in the distance
that they inspire you with fear. They seem to
be luminous of themselves, so vividly do they
stand out in their clear rose against the deep
blue of the star-spangled vault. And this apparent radiation from within, by its lack of like-
lihood, makes them seem more awful.

And all around is the desert; a corner of the
mournful kingdom of sand. Nothing else is to
be seen anywhere save those three awful things
that stand there upright and still—the human
likeness magnified beyond all measurement, and
the three geometric mountains; things at first
sight like exhalations, visionary things, with
nevertheless here and there, and most of all in
the features of the vast mute face, subtleties of
shadow which show that *it* at least exists, rigid
and immovable, fashioned out of imperishable
stone.

Even had we not known, we must soon have
guessed, for these things are unique in the world,
and pictures of every age have made the knowledge of them commonplace: the Sphinx and
the Pyramids! But what is strange is that
they should be so disquieting. . . . And this per-

vading colour of rose, whence comes it, seeing
that usually the moon tints with blue the things
it illumines? One would not expect this colour
either, which, nevertheless, is that of all the
sands and all the granites of Egypt and Arabia.
And then too, the eyes of the statue, how often
had we not seen them? And did we not know
that they were capable only of their one fixed
stare? Why is it then that their motionless
regard surprises and chills us, even while we are
obsessed by the smile of the sealed lips that
seem to hold back the answer to the supreme
enigma? . . .

It is cold, but cold as in our country are the
fine nights of January, and a wintry mist rises
low down in the little valleys of the sand. And
that again we were not expecting; beyond
question the latest invaders of this country, by
changing the course of the old Nile, so as to
water the earth and make it more productive,
have brought hither the humidity of their own
misty isle. And this strange cold, this mist,
light as it still is, seem to presage the end of
ages, give an added remoteness and finality to
all this dead past, which lies here beneath us in
subterranean labyrinths haunted by a thousand
mummies.

And the mist, which, as the night advances,
thickens in the valleys, hesitates to mount to

the great daunting face of the Sphinx; and
covers it with the merest and most transparent
gauze; and, like everything else here to-night,
this gauze, too, is rose-coloured. And meanwhile the Sphinx, which has seen the unrolling
of all the history of the world, attends impas-
sively the change in Egypt's climate, plunged
in profound and mystic contemplation of the
moon, its friend for the last 5000 years.

Here and there on the soft pathway of the
sandhills are pigmy figures of men that move
about or sit squatting as if on the watch; and
small as they are, low down in the hollows
and far away, this wonderful silver moon reveals
even their slightest gestures; for their white robes
and black cloaks stand sharply out against the
monotonous rose of the desert. At times they
call to one another in a harsh, aspirate tongue,
and then go off at a run, noiselessly, barefooted,
with burnous flying, like moths in the night.
They lie in wait for the parties of tourists who
arrive from time to time. For the great symbols,
during the hundreds and thousands of years
that have elapsed since men ceased to venerate
them, have nevertheless scarcely ever been alone,
especially on nights with a full moon. Men
of all races, of all times, have come to wander
round them, vaguely attracted by their immensity and mystery. In the days of the Romans

they had already become symbols of a lost sig-
nificance, legacies of a fabulous antiquity, but
people came curiously to contemplate them, and
tourists in toga and in peplus carved their names
on the granite of their bases for the sake of re-
membrance.

The tourists who have come to-night, and upon
whom have pounced the black-cloaked Bedouin
guides, wear cap and ulster or furred greatcoat;
their intrusion here seems almost an offence;
but, alas, such visitors become more numerous in
each succeeding year. The great town hard by
—which sweats gold now that men have started
to buy from it its dignity and its soul—is become
a place of rendezvous and holiday for the idlers
and upstarts of the whole world. The modern
spirit encompasses the old desert of the Sphinx
on every side. It is true that up to the present
no one has dared to profane it by building in
the immediate neighbourhood of the great statue.
Its fixity and calm disdain still hold some sway,
perhaps. But little more than a mile away
there ends a road travelled by hackney carriages
and tramway cars, and noisy with the delectable
hootings of smart motor cars; and behind the
pyramid of Cheops squats a vast hotel to which
swarm men and women of fashion, the latter
absurdly feathered, like Redskins at a scalp
dance; and sick people, in search of purer air;

and consumptive English maidens; and ancient English dames, a little the worse for wear, who bring their rheumatisms for the treatment of the dry winds.

Passing on our way hither, we had seen this road and this hotel and these people in the glare of the electric lights, and from an orchestra that was playing there we caught the trivial air of a popular refrain of the music halls; but when in a dip of the ground all this had disappeared, what a sense of deliverance possessed us, how far off this turmoil seemed! As soon as we commenced to tread upon the sand of centuries, where all at once our footsteps made no sound, nothing seemed to have existence, save only the great calm and the religious awe of this world into which we were come, of this world with its so crushing commentary upon our own, where all seemed silent, undefined, gigantic and suffused with rose-colour.

And first there is the pyramid of Cheops, whose immutable base we had to skirt on our way hither. In the moonlight we could see the separate blocks, so enormous, so regular, so even in their layers, which lie one above the other to infinity, getting ever smaller and smaller, and mounting, mounting in diminishing perspective, until at last high up they form the apex of this giddy triangle. And the pyramid seemed

to be illumined by some sad dawn of the end of
the world, a dawn which made ruddy only the
sands and the granites of earth, and left the
heavens, pricked with their myriad stars, more
awful in their darkness. How impossible it is
for us to conceive the mental attitude of that
king who, during some half-century, spent the
lives of thousands and thousands of his slaves
in the construction of this tomb, in the fond
and foolish hope of prolonging to infinity the
existence of his mummy.

The pyramid once passed there was still a
short way to go before we confronted the Sphinx,
in the middle of what our contemporaries have
left him of his desert. We had to descend the
slope of that sandhill which looked like a cloud,
and seemed as if covered with felt, in order to
preserve in such a place a more complete silence.
And here and there we passed a gaping black
hole—an airhole, as it seemed, of the profound
and inextricable kingdom of mummies, very
populous still, in spite of the zeal of the
exhumers.

As we descended the sandy pathway we were
not slow to perceive the Sphinx itself, half hill,
half couchant beast, turning its back upon us in
the attitude of a gigantic dog, that thought
to bay the moon; its head stood out in dark
silhouette, like a screen before the light it seemed

to be regarding, and the lappets of its headgear showed like downhanging ears. And then
gradually, as we walked on, we saw it in profile,
shorn of its nose—flat-nosed like a death's head
—but having already an expression even when
seen afar off and from the side; already disdainful
with thrust-out chin and baffling, mysterious
smile. And when at length we arrived before
the colossal visage, face to face with it—without
however encountering its gaze, which passed high
above our heads—there came over us at once
the sentiment of all the secret thought which
these men of old contrived to incorporate and
make eternal behind this mutilated mask.

But in full daylight their great Sphinx is no
more. It has ceased as it were to exist. It is
so scarred by time, and by the hands of iconoclasts; so dilapidated, broken and diminished,
that it is as inexpressive as the crumbling
mummies found in the sarcophagi, which no
longer even ape humanity. But after the manner of all phantoms it comes to life again at
night, beneath the enchantments of the moon.

For the men of its time whom did it represent?
King Amenemhat? The Sun God? Who can
rightly tell? Of all hieroglyphic images it
remains the one least understood. The unfathomable thinkers of Egypt symbolised everything for the benefit of the uninitiated under the

form of awe-inspiring figures of the gods; and it
may be, perhaps, that, after having meditated so
deeply in the shadow of their temples, and sought
so long the everlasting wherefore of life and
death, they wished simply to sum up in the smile
of these closed lips the vanity of the most profound of our human speculations. . . . It is said
that the Sphinx was once of striking beauty,
when harmonious contour and colouring animated the face, and it was enthroned at its full
height on a kind of esplanade paved with long
slabs of stone. But was it then more sovereign
than it is to-night in its last decrepitude?
Almost buried beneath the sand of the Libyan
desert, which now quite hides its base, it rises at
this hour like a phantom which nothing solid
sustains in the air.

   .   .   .   .

It has gone midnight. In little groups the
tourists of the evening have disappeared; to
regain perhaps the neighbouring hotel, where
the orchestra doubtless has not ceased to rage;
or may be, remounting their cars, to join, in
some club of Cairo, one of those bridge parties,
in which the really superior intellects of our time
delight; some—the stouthearted ones—departed
talking loudly and with cigar in mouth; others,
however, daunted in spite of themselves, lowered
their voices as people instinctively do in church.

And the Bedouin guides, who a moment ago
seemed to flutter about the giant monument like
so many black moths—they too have gone,
made restless by the cold air, which erstwhile
they had not known. The show for to-night is
over, and everywhere silence reigns.

The rosy tint fades on the Sphinx and the
pyramids; all things in the ghostly scene grow
visibly paler; for the moon as it rises becomes
more silvery in the increasing chilliness of midnight. The winter mist, exhaled from the artificially watered fields below, continues to rise,
takes heart and envelops the great mute face
itself. And the latter persists in its regard of
the dead moon, preserving still the old disconcerting smile. It becomes more and more difficult
to believe that here before us is a real colossus,
so surely does it seem nothing other than a dilated
reflection of a thing which exists *elsewhere,* in
some other world. And behind in the distance
are the three triangular mountains. Them, too,
the fog envelops, till they also cease to exist, and
become pure visions of the Apocalypse.

Now it is that little by little an intolerable
sadness is expressed in those large eyes with
their empty sockets—for, at this moment, the
ultimate secret, that which the Sphinx seems to
have known for so many centuries, but to have
withheld in melancholy irony, is this: that all

these dead men and women who sleep in the vast necropolis below have been fooled, and the awakening signal has not sounded for a single one of them; and that the creation of mankind —mankind that thinks and suffers—has had no rational explanation, and that our poor aspirations are vain, but so vain as to awaken pity.

THE PASSING OF CAIRO

CHAPTER II

RAGGED, threatening clouds, like those that bring the showers of our early spring, hurry across a pale evening sky, whose mere aspect makes you cold. A wintry wind, raw and bitter, blows without ceasing, and brings with it every now and then some furtive spots of rain.

A carriage takes me towards what was once the residence of the great Mehemet Ali: by a steep incline it ascends into the midst of rocks and sand—and already, and almost in a moment, we seem to be in the desert; though we have scarcely left behind the last houses of an Arab quarter, where long-robed folk, who looked half-frozen, were muffled up to the eyes to-day. . . . Was there formerly such weather as this in this country noted for its unchanging mildness?

This residence of the great sovereign of Egypt, the citadel and the mosque which he had made for his last repose, are perched like eagles' nests on a spur of the mountain chain of Arabia, the Mokattam, which stretches out like a promontory towards the basin of the Nile, and brings quite close to Cairo, so as almost to over-

17

hang it, a little of the desert solitude. And so the eye can see from far off and from all sides the mosque of Mehemet Ali, with the flattened domes of its cupolas, its pointed minarets, its general aspect so entirely Turkish, perched high up, with a certain unexpectedness, above the Arab town which it dominates. The prince who sleeps there wished that it should resemble the mosques of his fatherland, and it looks as if it had been transported bodily from Stamboul.

A short trot brings us up to the lower gate of the old fortress; and, by a natural effect, as we ascend, all Cairo, which is near there, seems to rise with us: not yet indeed the endless multitude of its houses; but at first only the thousands of its minarets, which in a few seconds point their high towers into the mournful sky, and suggest at once that an immense town is about to unfold itself under our eyes.

Continuing to ascend—past the double rampart, the double or triple gates, which all these old fortresses possess, we penetrate at length into a large fortified courtyard, the crenellated walls of which shut out our further view. Soldiers are on guard there—and how unexpected are such soldiers in this holy place of Egypt! The red uniforms and the white faces of the north: Englishmen, billeted in the palace of Mehemet Ali!

The mosque first meets the eye, preceding the palace. And as we approach, it is Stamboul indeed—for me dear old Stamboul—which is called to mind; there is nothing, whether in the lines of its architecture or in the details of its ornamentation, to suggest the art of the Arabs —a purer art it may be than this and of which many excellent examples may be seen in Cairo. No; it is a corner of Turkey into which we are suddenly come.

Beyond a courtyard paved with marble, silent and enclosed, which serves as a vast parvis, the sanctuary recalls those of Mehmet Fatih or the Chah Zadé: the same sanctified gloom, into which the stained glass of the narrow windows casts a splendour as of precious stones; the same extreme distance between the enormous pillars, leaving more clear space than in our churches, and giving to the domes the appearance of being held up by enchantment.

The walls are of a strange white marble streaked with yellow. The ground is completely covered with carpets of a sombre red. In the vaults, very elaborately wrought, nothing but blacks and golds: a background of black bestrewn with golden roses, and bordered with arabesques like gold lace. And from above hang thousands of golden chains supporting the vigil lamps for the evening prayers. Here and there

are people on their knees, little groups in robe
and turban, scattered fortuitously upon the red
of the carpets, and almost lost in the midst of
the sumptuous solitude.

In an obscure corner lies Mehemet Ali,
the prince adventurous and chivalrous as some
legendary hero, and withal one of the greatest
sovereigns of modern history.   There he lies
behind a grating of gold, of complicated design,
in that Turkish style, already decadent, but still
so beautiful, which was that of his epoch.

Through the golden bars may be seen in the
shadow the catafalque of state, in three tiers,
covered with blue brocades, exquisitely faded,
and profusely embroidered with dull gold.   Two
long green palms freshly cut from some date-
tree in the neighbourhood are crossed before
the door of this sort of funeral enclosure.   And
it seems that around us is an inviolable religious
peace. . . .

But all at once there comes a noisy chattering
in a Teutonic tongue—and shouts and laughs!
. . . How is it possible, so near to the great
dead? . . . And there enters a group of tourists,
dressed more or less in the approved " smart "
style.   A guide, with a droll countenance,
recites to them the beauties of the place,
bellowing at the top of his voice like a show-
man at a fair.   And one of the travellers,

stumbling in the sandals which are too large for her small feet, laughs a prolonged, silly little laugh like the clucking of a turkey. . . .

Is there then no keeper, no guardian of this holy mosque? And amongst the faithful prostrate here in prayer, none who will rise and make indignant protest? Who after this will speak to us of the fanaticism of the Egyptians? . . . Too meek, rather, they seem to me everywhere. Take any church you please in Europe where men go down on their knees in prayer, and I should like to see what kind of a welcome would be accorded to a party of Moslem tourists who—to suppose the impossible—behaved so badly as these savages here.

Behind the mosque is an esplanade, and beyond that the palace. The palace, as such, can scarcely be said to exist any longer, for it has been turned into a barrack for the army of occupation. English soldiers, indeed, meet us at every turn, smoking their pipes in the idleness of the evening. One of them who does not smoke is trying to carve his name with a knife on one of the layers of marble at the base of the sanctuary.

At the end of this esplanade there is a kind of balcony from which one may see the whole of the town, and an unlimited extent of verdant plains and yellow desert. It is a favourite view of the tourists of the agencies, and we meet again our friends of the mosque, who have preceded us hither—the gentlemen with the loud voices, the bellowing guide and the cackling lady. Some soldiers are standing there too, smoking their pipes contemplatively. But in spite of all these people, in spite, too, of the wintry sky, the scene which presents itself on arrival there is ravishing.

A very fairyland—but a fairyland quite different from that of Stamboul. For whereas the latter is ranged like a great amphitheatre above the Bosphorus and the Sea of Marmora, here the vast town is spread out simply, in a plain surrounded by the solitude of the desert and dominated by chaotic rocks. Thousands of minarets rise up on every side like ears of corn in a field; far away in the distance one can see their innumerable slender points—but instead of being simply, as at Stamboul, so many white spires, they are here complicated by arabesques, by galleries, clock-towers and little columns, and seem to have borrowed the reddish colour of the desert.

The flat roofs tell of a region which formerly was without rain. The innumerable palm-trees of the gardens, above this ocean of mosques and houses, sway their plumes in the wind, bewildered as it were by these clouds laden with cold showers. In the south and in the west, at the extreme limits of the view, as if upon the misty horizon of the plains, appear two gigantic triangles. They are Gizeh and Memphis—the eternal pyramids.

At the north of the town there is a corner of the desert quite singular in its character— of the colour of bistre and of mummy—where a whole colony of high cupolas, scattered at random, still stand upright in the midst of sand and desolate rocks. It is the proud cemetery of the Mameluke Sultans, whose day was done in the Middle Ages.

But if one looks closely, what disorder, what a mass of ruins there are in this town—still a little fairylike — beaten this evening by the squalls of winter. The domes, the holy tombs, the minarets and terraces, all are crumbling: the hand of death is upon them all. But down there, in the far distance, near to that silver streak which meanders through the plains, and which is the old Nile, the advent of new times is proclaimed by the chimneys of factories, impudently high, that disfigure everything, and spout forth into the twilight thick clouds of black smoke.

The night is falling as we descend from the esplanade to return to our lodgings.

We have first to traverse the old town of

Cairo, a maze of streets still full of charm, wherein the thousand little lamps of the Arab shops already shed their quiet light. Passing through streets which twist at their caprice, beneath overhanging balconies covered with wooden trellis of exquisite workmanship, we have to slacken speed in the midst of a dense crowd of men and beasts. Close to us pass women, veiled in black, gently mysterious as in the olden times, and men of unmoved gravity, in long robes and white draperies; and little donkeys pompously bedecked in collars of blue beads; and rows of leisurely camels, with their loads of lucerne, which exhale the pleasant fragrance of the fields. And when in the gathering gloom, which hides the signs of decay, there appear suddenly, above the little houses, so lavishly ornamented with mushrabiyas and arabesques, the tall aerial minarets, rising to a prodigious height into the twilight sky, it is still the adorable East.

But nevertheless, what ruins, what filth, what rubbish! How present is the sense of impending dissolution! And what is this: large pools of water in the middle of the road! Granted that there is more rain here than formerly, since the valley of the Nile has been artificially irrigated, it still seems almost impossible that there should be all this black water, into which our carriage sinks to the very axles; for it is a clear week since any serious quantity of rain fell. It would seem that the new masters of this land, albeit the cost of annual upkeep has risen in their hands to the sum of £15,000,000, have given no thought to drainage. But the good Arabs, patiently and without murmuring, gather up their long robes, and with legs bare to the knee make their way through this already pestilential water, which must be hatching for them fever and death.

Farther on, as the carriage proceeds on its course, the scene changes little by little. The streets become vulgar: the houses of "The Arabian Nights" give place to tasteless Levantine buildings; electric lamps begin to pierce the darkness with their wan, fatiguing glare, and at a sharp turning the new Cairo is before us.

What is this? Where are we fallen? Save that it is more vulgar, it might be Nice, or the Riviera, or Interlaken, or any other of those towns of carnival whither the bad taste of the whole world comes to disport itself in the so-called fashionable seasons. But in these quarters, on the other hand, which belong to the foreigners and to the Egyptians rallied to the civilisation of the West, all is clean and dry, well cared for and well kept. There are no ruts, no refuse. The fifteen million pounds have done their work conscientiously.

Everywhere is the blinding glare of the electric light; monstrous hotels parade the sham splendour of their painted façades; the whole length of the streets is one long triumph of imitation, of mud walls plastered so as to look like stone; a medley of all styles, rockwork, Roman, Gothic, New Art, Pharaonic, and, above all, the pretentious and the absurd. Innumerable public houses overflow with bottles; every alcoholic drink, all the poisons of the West, are here turned into Egypt with a take-what-you-please.

And taverns, gambling-dens and houses of ill-fame. And parading the side-walks, numerous Levantine damsels, who seek by their finery to imitate their fellows of the Paris boulevards, but who by mistake, as we must suppose, have placed their orders with some costumier for performing dogs.

This then is the Cairo of the future, this cosmopolitan fair! Good heavens! When will the Egyptians recollect themselves, when will they realise that their forebears have left to them an inalienable patrimony of art, of architecture and exquisite refinement; and that, by their negligence, one of those towns which used to be the most beautiful in the world is falling into ruin and about to perish?

And nevertheless amongst the young Moslems and Copts now leaving the schools there are so many of distinguished mind and superior intelligence! When I see the things that are here, see them with the fresh eyes of a stranger, landed but yesterday upon this soil, impregnated with the glory of antiquity, I want to cry out to them, with a frankness that is brutal perhaps, but with a profound sympathy:

" Bestir yourselves before it is too late. Defend yourselves against this disintegrating invasion—not by force, be it understood, not by inhospitality or ill-humour — but by disdaining this Occidental rubbish, this last year's frippery by which you are inundated. Try to preserve not only your traditions and your admirable Arab language, but also the grace and mystery that used to characterise your town, the refined luxury of your dwelling-houses. It is not a question now of a poet's fancy; your national dignity is at stake. You are *Orientals*—I pronounce respectfully that word, which implies a whole past of early civilisation, of unmingled greatness—but in a few years, unless you are on your guard, you will have become mere Levantine brokers, exclusively preoccupied with the price of land and the rise in cotton."

THE MOSQUES OF CAIRO

CHAPTER III

THEY are almost innumerable, more than 3000, and this great town, which covers some twelve miles of plain, might well be called a city of mosques. (I speak, of course, of the ancient Cairo, of the Cairo of the Arabs. The new Cairo, the Cairo of sham elegance and of "Semiramis Hotels," does not deserve to be mentioned except with a smile.)

A city of mosques, then, as I was saying. They follow one another along the streets, sometimes two, three, four in a row; leaning one against the other, so that their confines become merged. On all sides their minarets shoot up into the air, those minarets embellished with arabesques, carved and complicated with the most changing fancy. They have their little balconies, their rows of little columns; they are so fashioned that the daylight shows through them. Some are far away in the distance; others quite close, pointing straight into the sky above our heads. No matter where one looks—as far as the eye can see—still there are others; all of the same familiar colour, a brown turning into rose. The most ancient of them, those of the old easy-tempered times, bristle with shafts of wood, placed there as resting places for the great free birds of the air, and vultures and ravens may always be seen perched there, contemplating the horizon of the sands, the line of the yellow solitudes.

Three thousand mosques! Their great straight walls, a little severe perhaps, and scarcely pierced by their tiny ogive windows, rise above the height of the neighbouring houses. These walls are of the same brown colour as the minarets, except that they are painted with horizontal stripes of an old red, which has been faded by the sun; and they are crowned invariably with a series of trefoils, after the fashion of battlements, but trefoils which in every case are different and surprising.

Before the mosques, which are raised like altars, there is always a flight of steps with a balustrade of white marble. From the door one gets a glimpse of the calm interior in deep shadow. Once inside there are corridors, astonishingly lofty, sonorous and enveloped in a kind of half gloom; immediately on entering one experiences a sense of coolness and pervading peace; they prepare you as it were, and you begin to be filled with a spirit of devotion, and instinctively to speak low. In the narrow

street outside there was the clamorous uproar
of an Oriental crowd, cries of sellers, and the
noise of humble old-world trading; men and
beasts jostled you; there seemed a scarcity of
air beneath those so numerous overhanging
mushrabiyas.   But here suddenly there is silence, broken only by the vague murmur of
prayers and the sweet songs of birds; there is
silence too, and the sense of open space, in the
holy garden enclosed within high walls; and
again in the sanctuary, resplendent in its quiet
and restful magnificence.   Few people as a rule
frequent the mosques, except of course at the
hours of the five services of the day.   In a few
chosen corners, particularly cool and shady,
some greybeards isolate themselves to read from
morning till night the holy books and to ponder
the thought of approaching death: they may be
seen there in their white turbans, with their white
beards and grave faces.   And there may be, too,
some few poor homeless outcasts, who are come
to seek the hospitality of Allah, and sleep,
careless of the morrow, stretched to their full
length on mats.

The peculiar charm of the gardens of the
mosques, which are often very extensive, is that
they are so jealously enclosed within their high
walls — crowned always with stone trefoils —
which completely shut out the hubbub of the

outer world.   Palm-trees, which have grown
there for some hundred years perhaps, rise from
the ground, either separately or in superb
clusters, and temper the light of the always hot
sun on the rose-trees and the flowering hibiscus.
There is no noise in the gardens, any more than
in the cloisters, for people walk there in sandals
and with measured tread.   And there are Edens,
too, for the birds, who live and sing therein in
complete security, even during the services,
attracted by the little troughs which the imams
fill for their benefit each morning with water
from the Nile.

As for the mosque itself it is rarely closed on
all sides as are those in the countries of the more
sombre Islam of the north.   Here in Egypt
—since there is no real winter and scarcely ever
any rain—one of the sides of the mosque is left
completely open to the garden; and the sanctuary is separated from the verdure and the roses
only by a simple colonnade.   Thus the faithful
grouped beneath the palm-trees can pray there
equally as well as in the interior of the mosque,
since they can see, between the arches, the
holy Mihrab.[1]

[1] The Mihrab is a kind of portico indicating the direction of
Mecca.   It is placed at the end of each mosque, as the altar is
in our churches, and the faithful are supposed to face it when
they pray.

Oh! this sanctuary seen from the silent garden, this sanctuary in which the pale gold gleams on the old ceiling of cedarwood, and mosaics of mother-of-pearl shine on the walls as if they were embroideries of silver that had been hung there.

There is no faience as in the mosques of Turkey or of Iran. Here it is the triumph of patient mosaic. Mother-of-pearl of all colours, all kinds of marble and of porphyry, cut into myriads of little pieces, precise and equal, and put together again to form the Arab designs, which, never borrowing from the human form, nor indeed from the form of any animal, recall rather those infinitely varied crystals that may be seen under the microscope in a flake of snow. It is always the Mihrab which is decorated with the most elaborate richness; generally little columns of lapis lazuli, intensely blue, rise in relief from it, framing mosaics so delicate that they look like brocades or fine lace. In the old ceilings of cedarwood, where the singing birds of the neighbourhood have their nests, the golds mingle with some most exquisite colourings, which time has taken care to soften and to blend together. And here and there very fine and long consoles of sculptured wood seem to fall, as it were, from the beams and hang upon the walls like stalactites; and these consoles, too, in past

times, have been carefully coloured and gilded.
As for the columns, always dissimilar, some of
amaranth-coloured marble, others of dark green,
others again of red porphyry, with capitals of
every conceivable style, they are come from far,
from the night of the ages, from the religious
struggles of an earlier time and testify to the
prodigious past which this valley of the Nile,
narrow as it is, and encompassed by the desert,
has known. They were formerly perhaps in the
temples of the pagans, or have known the strange
faces of the gods of Egypt and of ancient Greece
and Rome; they have been in the churches of
the early Christians, or have seen the statues of
tortured martyrs, and the images of the trans-
figured Christ, crowned with the Byzantine
aureole. They have been present at battles, at
the downfall of kingdoms, at hecatombs, at sacri-
leges; and now brought together promiscuously
in these mosques, they behold on the walls
of the sanctuary simply the thousand little
designs, ideally pure, of that Islam which wishes
that men when they pray should conceive Allah
as immaterial, a Spirit without form and without
feature.

Each one of these mosques has its sainted
dead, whose name it bears, and who sleeps by its
side, in an adjoining mortuary kiosk; some priest
rendered admirable by his virtues, or perhaps a

khedive of earlier times, or a soldier, or a martyr.
And the mausoleum, which communicates with
the sanctuary by means of a long passage, sometimes open, sometimes covered with gratings, is
surmounted always by a special kind of cupola,
a very high and curious cupola, which raises
itself into the sky like some gigantic dervish hat.
Above the Arab town, and even in the sand of
the neighbouring desert, these funeral domes
may be seen on every side adjoining the old
mosques to which they belong. And in the
evening, when the light is failing, they suggest
the odd idea that it is the dead man himself,
immensely magnified, who stands there beneath
a hat that is become immense. One can pray,
if one wishes, in this resting place of the dead
saint as well as in the mosque. Here indeed
it is always more secluded and more in shadow.
It is more simple, too, at least up to the height of
a man: on a platform of white marble, more or
less worn and yellowed by the touch of pious
hands, nothing more than an austere catafalque
of similar marble, ornamented merely with a
Cufic inscription. But if you raise your eyes to
look at the interior of the dome—the inside, as
it were, of the strange dervish hat—you will see
shining between the clusters of painted and
gilded stalactites a number of windows of exquisite colouring, little windows that seem to be

constellations of emeralds and rubies and sap-
phires. And the birds, you may be sure, have
their nests also in the house of the holy one.
They are wont indeed to soil the carpets and
the mats on which the worshippers kneel, and
their nests are so many blots up there amid
the gildings of the carved cedarwood; but then
their song, the symphony that issues from that
aviary, is so sweet to the living who pray and to
the dead who dream. . . .

.   .   .   .

But yet, when all is said, these mosques seem
somehow to be wanting. They do not wholly
satisfy you. The access to them perhaps is too
easy, and one feels too near to the modern
quarters of the town, where the hotels are full
of visitors—so that at any moment, it seems,
the spell may be broken by the entry of a batch
of Cook's tourists, armed with the inevitable
Baedeker. Alas! they are the mosques of
Cairo, of poor Cairo, that is invaded and profaned. The memory turns to those of Morocco,
so jealously guarded, to those of Persia, even
to those of Old Stamboul, where the shroud of
Islam envelops you in silence and gently bows
your shoulders as soon as you cross their
thresholds.

And yet what pains are being taken to-day
to preserve these mosques, which in olden times

were such delightful retreats.   Neglected for
whole centuries, never repaired, notwithstanding
the veneration of their heedless worshippers, the
greater part of them were fallen into ruin; the
fine woodwork of their interiors had become
worm-eaten, their cupolas were cracked and
their mosaics covered the floor as with a hail
of mother-of-pearl, of porphyry and marble.   It
seemed that to repair all this was a task in-
capable of fulfilment; it was sheer folly, people
said, to conceive the idea of it.

Nevertheless, for nearly twenty years now an
army of workers has been at the task, sculptors,
marble-cutters, mosaicists.   Already certain of
the sanctuaries, the most venerable of them
indeed, have been entirely renovated.   After
having re-echoed for some years to the sounds
of hammers and chisels, during the course of
these vast renovations, they are restored now
to peace and to prayer, and the birds have re-
commenced to build their nests in them.

It will be the glory of the present reign that
it has preserved, before it was too late, all this
magnificent legacy of Moslem art.   When
the city of " The Arabian Nights," which was
formerly here, shall have entirely disappeared, to
give place to a vulgar *entrepôt* of commerce and
of pleasure, to which the plutocracy of the whole
world comes every winter to disport itself, so

much at least will remain to bear testimony to
the lofty and magnificent thought that inspired
the earlier Arab life. These mosques will continue to remain into the distant future, even
when men shall have ceased to pray in them,
and the winged guests shall have departed, for
the want of those troughs of water from the
Nile, filled for them by the good imams, whose
hospitality they repay by making heard in the
courts, beneath the arched roofs, beneath the
ceilings of cedarwood, the sweet, piping music
of birds.

THE HALL OF
THE MUMMIES

CHAPTER IV

THE HALL OF THE MUMMIES

THERE are two of us, and as we light our way
by the aid of a lantern through these vast halls
we might be taken for a night watch on its
round. We have just shut behind us and
doubly locked the door by which we entered,
and we know that we are alone, rigorously
alone, although this place is so vast, with its
endless, communicating halls, its high vestibules
and great flights of stairs; mathematically alone,
one might almost say, for this palace that we
are in is one quite out of the ordinary, and all
its outlets were closed and sealed at nightfall.
Every night indeed the doors are sealed, on
account of the priceless relics that are collected
here. So we shall not meet with any living
being in these halls to-night, spite of their vast
extent and endless turnings, and in spite too
of all these mysterious things that are ranged
on every side and fill the place with shadows
and hiding places.

Our round takes us first along the ground
floor over flagstones that resound to our footsteps. It is about ten of the clock. Here and

43

there through some stray window gleams a small
patch of luminous blue sky, lit by the stars
which for the good folk outside lend transparency to the night; but here, none the less,
the place is filled with a solemn gloom, and we
lower our voices, remembering perhaps the dead
that fill the glass cases in the halls above.

And these things which line the walls on
either side of us as we pass also seem to be
in the nature of receptacles for the dead. For
the most part they are sarcophagi of granite,
proud and indestructible: some of them, in
the shape of gigantic boxes, are laid out in line
on pedestals; others, in the form of mummies,
stand upright against the walls and display
enormous faces, surmounted by equally enormous
head-dresses. Assembled there they look like
a lot of malformed giants, with oversized heads
sunk curiously in their shoulders. There are,
besides, some that are merely statues, colossal
figures that have never held a corpse in their
interiors; these all wear a strange, scarcely perceptible smile; in their huge sphinxlike headgear they reach nearly to the ceiling and their
set stare passes high above our heads. And
there are others that are not larger than ourselves, some even quite little, with the stature
of gnomes. And, every now and then, at some
sudden turning, we encounter a pair of eyes of

enamel, wide-open eyes, that pierce straight into
the depths of ours, that seem to follow us as we
pass and make us shiver as if by the contact
of a thought that comes from the abysm of the
ages.

We pass on rapidly, however, and somewhat
inattentively, for our business here to-night is
not with these simulacra on the ground floor,
but with the more redoubtable hosts above.
Besides our lantern sheds so little light in these
great halls that all these people of granite and
sandstone and marble appear only at the precise
moment of our passage, appear only to disappear, and, spreading their fantastic shadows
on the walls, mingle the next moment with
the great mute crowd, that grows ever more
numerous behind us.

Placed at intervals are apparatus for use in
case of fire, coils of hose and standpipes that
shine with the warm glow of burnished copper,
and I ask my companion of the watch: "What
is there that could burn here? Are not these
good people all of stone?" And he answers:
"Not here indeed; but consider how the things
that are above would blaze." Ah! yes. The
"things that are above"—which are indeed the
object of my visit to-night. I had not thought
of fire catching hold in an assembly of mummies;
of the old withered flesh, the dead, dry hair, the

venerable carcasses of kings and queens, soaked
as they are in natron and oils, crackling like so
many boxes of matches. It is chiefly on account
of this danger indeed that the seals are put upon
the doors at nightfall, and that it needs a special
favour to be allowed to penetrate into this place
at night with a lantern.

In the daytime this "Museum of Egyptian
Antiquities" is as vulgar a thing as you can
conceive, filled though it is with priceless
treasures. It is the most pompous, the most
outrageous of those buildings, of no style at all,
by which each year the New Cairo is enriched;
open to all who care to gaze at close quarters, in
a light that is almost brutal, upon these august
dead, who fondly thought that they had hidden
themselves for ever.

But at night! . . . Ah! at night when all the
doors are closed, it is the palace of nightmare
and of fear.   At night, so say the Arab guardians,
who would not enter it at the price of gold—no,
not even after offering up a prayer—at night,
horrible " forms " escape, not only from the embalmed bodies that sleep in the glass cases above,
but also from the great statues, from the papyri,
and the thousand and one things that, at the
bottom of the tombs, have long been impregnated
with human essence.   And these " forms " are
like unto dead bodies, and sometimes to strange

beasts, even to beasts that crawl. And, after having wandered about the halls, they end by assembling for their nocturnal conferences on the roofs.

We next ascend a staircase of monumental proportions, empty in its whole extent, where we are delivered for a little while from the obsession of those rigid figures, from the stares and smiles of the good people in white stone and black granite who throng the galleries and vestibules on the ground floor. None of them, to be sure, will follow us; but all the same they guard in force and perplex with their shadows the only way by which we can retreat, if the formidable hosts above have in store for us too sinister a welcome.

He to whose courtesy I owe the relaxation of the orders of the night is the illustrious savant to whose care has been entrusted the direction of the excavations in Egyptian soil; he is also the comptroller of this vast museum, and it is he himself who has kindly consented to act as my guide to-night through its mazy labyrinth.

Across the silent halls above we now proceed straight towards those of whom I have demanded this nocturnal audience.

To-night the succession of these rooms, filled with glass cases, which cover more than four hundred yards along the four sides of the building, seems to be without end. After passing, in turn, the papyri, the enamels, the vases that contain human entrails, we reach the mummies of the sacred beasts: cats, ibises, dogs, hawks, all with their mummy cloths and sarcophagi; and monkeys, too, that remain grotesque even in death. Then commence the human masks, and, upright in glass-fronted cupboards, the mummy cases in which the body, swathed in its mummy cloths, was moulded, and which reproduced, more or less enlarged, the figure of the deceased. Quite a lot of courtesans of the Greco-Roman epoch, moulded in paste in this wise after death and crowned with roses, smile at us provokingly from behind their windows. Masks of the colour of dead flesh alternate with others of gold which gleam as the light of our lantern plays upon them momentarily in our rapid passage. Their eyes are always too large, the eyelids too wide open and the dilated pupils seem to stare at us with alarm. Amongst these mummy cases and these coffin lids fashioned in the shape of the human figure, there are some that seem to have been made for giants; the head especially, beneath its cumbrous head-dress the head stuffed as it were between the hunch-back shoulders, looks enormous, out of all proportion to the body which, towards the feet, narrows like a scabbard.

Although our little lantern maintains its light we seem to see here less and less: the darkness around us in these vast rooms becomes almost overpowering—and these are the rooms, too, that, leading one into the other, facilitate the midnight promenade of those dread " forms " which, every evening, are released and roam about. . . .

On a table in the middle of one of these rooms a thing to make you shudder gleams in a glass box, a fragile thing that failed of life some two thousand years ago.   It is the mummy of a human embryo, and someone, to appease the malice of this born-dead thing, had covered its face with a coating of gold—for, according to the belief of the Egyptians, these little abortions became the evil genii of their families if proper honour was not paid to them.   At the end of its negligible body, the gilded head, with its great fœtus eyes, is unforgettable for its suffering ugliness, for its frustrated and ferocious expression.

In the halls into which we next penetrate there are veritable dead bodies ranged on either side of us as we pass; their coffins are displayed in tiers one above the other; the air is heavy with the sickly odour of mummies; and on the ground, curled always like some huge serpent, the leather hoses are in readiness, for here indeed is the danger spot for fire.

And the master of this strange house whispers

to me: "This is the place. Look! There they are."

In truth I recognise the place, having often come here in the daytime, like other people. In spite of the darkness, which commences at some ten paces from us—so small is the circle of light cast by our lantern—I can distinguish the double row of the great royal coffins, open without shame in their glass cases. And standing against the walls, upright, like so many sentinels, are the coffin lids, fashioned in the shape of the human figure.

We are there at last, admitted at this unseasonable hour into the guest-chamber of kings and queens, for an audience that is private indeed.

And there, first of all, is the woman with the baby, upon whom, without stopping, we throw the light of our lantern. A woman who died in giving to the world a little dead prince. Since the old embalmers no one has seen the face of this Queen Makeri. In her coffin there she is simply a tall female figure, outlined beneath the close-bound swathings of brown-coloured bandages. At her feet lies the fatal baby, grotesquely shrivelled, and veiled and mysterious as the mother herself; a sort of doll, it seems, put there to keep her eternal company in the slow passing of endless years.

More fearsome to approach is the row of unswathed mummies that follow. Here, in each coffin over which we bend, there is a face which stares at us—or else closes its eyes in order that it may not see us; and meagre shoulders and lean arms, and hands with overgrown nails that protrude from miserable rags. And each royal mummy that our lantern lights reserves for us a fresh surprise and the shudder of a different fear —they resemble one another so little. Some of them seem to laugh, showing their yellow teeth; others have an expression of infinite sadness and suffering. Sometimes the faces are small, refined and still beautiful despite the pinching of the nostrils; sometimes they are excessively enlarged by putrid swelling, with the tip of the nose eaten away. The embalmers, we know, were not sure of their means, and the mummies were not always a success. In some cases putrefaction ensued, and corruption and even sudden hatchings of larvæ, those " companions without ears and without eyes," which died indeed in time but only after they had perforated all the flesh.

Hard by are ranked according to dynasty, and in chronological order, the proud Pharaohs in a piteous row: father, son, grandson, great-grandson. And common paper tickets tell their tremendous names, Seti I., Ramses II., Seti II., Ramses III., Ramses IV. . . . Soon the muster will be complete, with such energy have men dug in the heart of the rocks to find them all; and these glass cases will no doubt be their final resting place. In olden days, however, they made many pilgrimages after their death, for in the troubled times of the history of Egypt it was one of the harassing preoccupations of the reigning sovereign to hide, to hide at all costs, the mummies of his ancestors, which filled the earth increasingly, and which the violators of tombs were so swift to track. Then they were carried clandestinely from one grave to another, raised each from his own pompous sepulchre, to be buried at last together in some humble and less conspicuous vault. But it is here, in this museum of Egyptian antiquities, that they are about to accomplish their return to dust, which has been deferred, as if by miracle, for so many centuries. Now, stripped of their bandages, their days are numbered, and it behoves us to hasten to draw these physiognomies of three or four thousand years ago, which are about to perish.

In that coffin—the last but one of the row on the left—it is the great Sesostris himself who awaits us. We know of old that face of ninety years, with its nose hooked like the beak of a falcon; and the gaps between those old man's teeth; the meagre, birdlike neck, and the hand

raised in a gesture of menace. Twenty years have
elapsed since he was brought back to the light,
this master of the world. He was wrapped
thousands of times in a marvellous winding-sheet,
woven of aloe fibres, finer than the muslin of
India, which must have taken years in the
making and measured more than 400 yards
in length. The unswathing, done in the presence of the Khedive Tewfik and the great per-
sonages of Egypt, lasted two hours, and after
the last turn, when the illustrious figure appeared, the emotion amongst the assistants was
such that they stampeded like a herd of cattle,
and the Pharaoh was overturned. He has,
moreover, given much cause for conversation,
this great Sesostris, since his installation in the
museum. Suddenly one day with a brusque
gesture, in the presence of the attendants, who
fled howling with fear, he raised that hand which
is still in the air, and which he has not deigned
since to lower.[1] And subsequently there super-
vened, beginning in the old yellowish-white
hair, and then swarming over the whole body,
a hatching of cadaveric fauna, which necessitated
a complete bath in mercury. He also has his
paper ticket, pasted on the end of his box, and

[1] This movement is explained by the action of the sun, which,
falling on the unclothed arm, is supposed to have expanded
the bone of the elbow.

one may read there, written in a careless hand,
that name which once caused the whole world
to tremble—" Ramses II. (Sesostris)"! It need
not be said that he has greatly fallen away and
blackened even in the fifteen years that I have
known him. He is a phantom that is about to
disappear; in spite of all the care lavished upon
him, a poor phantom about to fall to pieces,
to sink into nothingness. We move our lantern
about his hooked nose, the better to decipher,
in the play of shadow, his expression, that still
remains authoritative. . . . To think that once
the destinies of the world were ruled, without
appeal, by the nod of this head, which looks
now somewhat narrow, under the dry skin and
the horrible whitish hair. What force of will,
of passion and colossal pride must once have
dwelt therein! Not to mention the anxiety,
which to us now is scarcely conceivable, but
which in his time overmastered all others—the
anxiety, that is to say, of assuring the magnificence and inviolability of sepulture! . . . .
And this horrible scarecrow, toothless and senile,
lying here in its filthy rags, with the hand
raised in an impotent menace, was once the
brilliant Sesostris, the master of kings, and by
virtue of his strength and beauty the demigod
also, whose muscular limbs and deep athletic
chest many colossal statues at Memphis, at

Thebes, at Luxor, reproduce and try to make eternal. . . .

In the next coffin lies his father, Seti I., who reigned for a much shorter period, and died much younger than he. This youthfulness is apparent still in the features of the mummy, which are impressed besides with a persistent beauty. Indeed this good King Seti looks the picture of calm and serene reverie. There is nothing shocking in his dead face, with its long closed eyes, its delicate lips, its noble chin and unblemished profile. It is soothing and pleasant even to see him sleeping there with his hands crossed upon his breast. And it seems strange, that he, who looks so young, should have for son the old man, almost a centenarian, who lies beside him.

In our passage we have gazed on many other royal mummies, some tranquil and some grimacing. But, to finish, there is one of them (the third coffin there, in the row in front of us), a certain Queen Nsitanebashru, whom I approach with fear, albeit it is mainly on her account that I have ventured to make this fantastical round. Even in the daytime she attains to the maximum of horror that a spectral figure can evoke. What will she be like to-night in the uncertain light of our little lantern?

There she is indeed, the dishevelled vampire, in her place right enough, stretched at full length, but looking always as if she were about to leap up; and straightway I meet the sidelong glance of her enamelled pupils, shining out of half-closed eyelids, with lashes that are still almost perfect. Oh! the terrifying person! Not that she is ugly, on the contrary we can see that she was rather pretty and was mummied young. What distinguishes her from the others is her air of thwarted anger, of fury, as it were, at being dead. The embalmers have coloured her very religiously, but the pink, under the action of the salts of the skin, has become decomposed here and there and given place to a number of green spots. Her naked shoulders, the height of the arms above the rags which were once her splendid shroud, have still a certain sleek roundness, but they, too, are stained with greenish and black splotches, such as may be seen on the skins of snakes. Assuredly no corpse, either here or elsewhere, has ever preserved such an expression of intense life, of ironical, implacable ferocity. Her mouth is twisted in a little smile of defiance; her nostrils pinched like those of a ghoul on the scent of blood, and her eyes seem to say to each one who approaches: " Yes, I am laid in my coffin; but you will very soon see I can get out of it." There is something confusing in the thought that the menace of this terrible expression, and this appearance of ill-restrained ferocity had endured for some hundreds of years before the commencement of our era, and endured to no purpose in the secret darkness of a closed coffin at the bottom of some doorless vault.

Now that we are about to retire, what will happen here, with the complicity of silence, in the darkest hours of the night? Will they remain inert and rigid, all these embalmed bodies, once left to themselves, who pretended to be so quiet because we were there? What exchanges of old human fluid will recommence, as who can doubt they do each night between one coffin and another. Formerly these kings and queens, in their anxiety as to the future of their mummy, had foreseen violation, pillage and scattering amongst the sands of the desert, but never this: that they would be reunited one day, almost all unveiled, so near to one another under panes of glass. Those who governed Egypt in the lost centuries and were never known except by history, by the papyri inscribed with hieroglyphics, brought thus together, how many things will they have to say to one another, how many ardent questions to ask about their loves, about their crimes! As soon as we shall have departed, nay, as soon as our lantern, at the end of the long galleries, shall seem no more than a foolish, vanishing spot of fire, will not the " forms," of whom the attendants are so afraid, will they not start their nightly rumblings and in their hollow mummy voices, whisper, with difficulty, words? . . .

Heavens! How dark it is! Yet our lantern has not gone out. But it seems to grow darker and darker. And at night, when all is shut up, how one smells the odour of the oils in which the shrouds are saturated, and, more intolerable still, the sickly stealthy stench, almost, of all these dead bodies! . . .

As I traverse the obscurity of these endless halls, a vague instinct of self-preservation induces me to turn back again, and look behind. And it seems to me that already the woman with the baby is slowly raising herself, with a thousand precautions and stratagems, her head still completely covered. While farther down, that dishevelled hair. . . . Oh! I can see her well, sitting up with a sudden jerk, the ghoul with the enamel eyes, the lady Nsitanebashru!

A CENTRE OF ISLAM

CHAPTER V

" To learn is the duty of every Moslem."
Verse from the Hadith or Words of the Prophet.

In a narrow street, hidden in the midst of the most ancient Arab quarters of Cairo, in the very heart of a close labyrinth mysteriously shady, an exquisite doorway opens into a wide space bathed in sunshine; a doorway formed of two elaborate arches, and surmounted by a high frontal on which intertwined arabesques form wonderful rosework, and holy writings are enscrolled with the most ingenious complications.

It is the entrance to El-Azhar, a venerable place in Islam, whence have issued for nearly a thousand years the generations of priests and doctors charged with the propagation of the word of the Prophet amongst the nations, from the Mohreb to the Arabian Sea, passing through the great deserts. About the end of our tenth century the glorious Fatimee Caliphs built this immense assemblage of arches and columns, which became the seat of the most renowned

Moslem university in the world. And since
then successive sovereigns of Egypt have vied
with one another in perfecting and enlarging it;
adding new halls, new galleries, new minarets,
till they have made of El-Azhar almost a town
within a town.

.   .   .   .

"He who seeks instruction is more loved of God than he
who fights in a holy war."

A verse from the Hadith.

Eleven o'clock on a day of burning sunshine
and dazzling light. El-Azhar still vibrates with
the murmur of many voices, although the lessons
of the morning are nearly finished.

Once past the threshold of the double ornamented door we enter the courtyard, at this
moment empty as the desert and dazzling with
sunshine. Beyond, quite open, the mosque
spreads out its endless arcades, which are continued and repeated till they are lost in the
gloom of the far interior, and in this dim place,
with its perplexing depths, innumerable people
in turbans, sitting in a close crowd, are singing,
or rather chanting, in a low voice, and marking
time as it were to their declamation by a slight
rhythmic swaying from the hips. They are the
ten thousand students come from all parts of
the world to absorb the changeless doctrine of
El-Azhar.

At the first view it is difficult to distinguish them, for they are far down in the shadow, and out here we are almost blinded by the sun. In little attentive groups of from ten to twenty, seated on mats around a grave professor, they docilely repeat their lessons, which in the course of centuries have grown old without changing like Islam itself. And we wonder how those in the circles down there, in the aisles at the bottom where the daylight scarcely penetrates, can see to read the old difficult writings in the pages of their books.

In any case, let us not trouble them—as so many tourists nowadays do not hesitate to do; we will enter a little later, when the studies of the morning are over.

This court, upon which the sun of the forenoon now pours its white fire, is an enclosure severely and magnificently Arab; it has isolated us suddenly from time and things; it must lend to the Moslem prayer what formerly our Gothic churches lent to the Christian. It is vast as a tournament list; confined on one side by the mosque itself, and on the others by a high wall which effectively separates it from the outer world. The walls are of a reddish hue, burnt by centuries of sun into the colour of raw sienna or of bloodstone. At the bottom they are straight, simple, a little forbidding in their austerity, but

their summits are elaborately ornamented and
crowned with battlements, which show in profile
against the sky a long series of denticulated
stonework. And over this sort of reddish fret-
work of the top, which seems as if it were there
as a frame to the deep blue vault above us, we
see rising up distractedly all the minarets of the
neighbourhood; and these minarets are red-
coloured too, redder even than the jealous walls,
and are decorated with arabesques, pierced by
the daylight and complicated with aerial galleries. Some of them are a little distance
away; others, startlingly close, seem to scale the
zenith; and all are ravishing and strange, with
their shining crescents and outstretched shafts
of wood that call to the great birds of space.
Spite of ourselves we raise our heads, fascinated
by all the beauty that is in the air; but there
is only this square of marvellous sky, a sort
of limpid sapphire, set in the battlements of
El - Azhar and fringed by those audacious
slender towers. We are in the religious East
of olden days and we feel how the mystery
of this magnificent court—whose architectural
ornament consists merely in geometrical designs repeated to infinity, and does not commence till quite high up on the battlements,
where the minarets point into the eternal blue
—must cast its spell upon the imagination

of the young priests who are being trained here.

.   .   .   .

"He who instructs the ignorant is like a living man amongst the dead."

"If a day passes without my having learnt something which brings me nearer to God, let not the dawn of that day be blessed."

Verses from the Hadith.

He who has brought me to this place to-day is my friend, Mustapha Kamel Pacha,[1] the tribune of Egypt, and I owe to his presence the fact that I am not treated like a casual visitor. Our names are taken at once to the great master of El-Azhar, a high personage in Islam, whose pupil Mustapha formerly was, and who no doubt will receive us in person.

It is in a hall very Arab in its character, furnished only with divans, that the great master welcomes us, with the simplicity of an ascetic and the elegant manners of a prelate. His look, and indeed his whole face, tell how onerous is the sacred office which he exercises: to preside, namely, at the instruction of these thousands of young priests, who afterwards are to carry faith and peace and immobility to more than three hundred millions of men.

And in a few moments Mustapha and he are

[1] This happened a year before the death of the pacha to whom this book is dedicated.—*Author's Note.*

busy discussing—as if it were a matter of actual interest—a controversial question concerning the events which followed the death of the Prophet, and the part played by Ali. . . . In that moment how my good friend Mustapha, whom I had seen so French in France, appeared all at once a Moslem to the bottom of his soul! The same thing is true indeed of the greater number of these Orientals, who, if we meet them in our own country, seem to be quite parisianised; their modernity is only on the surface: in their inmost souls Islam remains intact. And it is not difficult to understand, perhaps, how the spectacle of our troubles, our despairs, our miseries, in these new ways in which our lot is cast, should make them reflect and turn again to the tranquil dream of their ancestors. . . .

While waiting for the conclusion of the morning studies, we are conducted through some of the dependencies of El-Azhar. Halls of every epoch, added one to another, go to form a little labyrinth; many contain *Mihrabs,* which, as we know already, are a kind of portico, festooned and denticulated till they look as if covered with rime. And library after library, with ceilings of cedarwood, carved in times when men had more leisure and more patience. Thousands of precious manuscripts, dating back some hundreds of years, but which here in El-Azhar are no whit out of date. Open, in glass cases, are numerous inestimable Korans, which in olden times had been written fair and illuminated on parchment by pious khedives. And, in a place of honour, a large astronomical glass, through which men watch the rising of the moon of Ramadan. . . . All this savours of the past. And what is being taught to-day to the ten thousand students of El-Azhar scarcely differs from what was taught to their predecessors in the glorious reign of the Fatimites—and which was then transcendent and even new: the Koran and all its commentaries; the subtleties of syntax and of pronunciation; jurisprudence; calligraphy, which still is dear to the heart of Orientals; versification; and, last of all, mathematics, of which the Arabs were the inventors.

Yes, all this savours of the past, of the dust of remote ages. And though, assuredly, the priests trained in this thousand-year-old university may grow to men of rarest soul, they will remain, these calm and noble dreamers, merely laggards, safe in their shelter from the whirlwind which carries us along.

. . . .

"It is a sacrilege to prohibit knowledge. To seek knowledge is to perform an act of adoration towards God; to instruct is to do an act of charity."

"Knowledge is the life of Islam, the column of faith."

Verses from the Hadith.

The lesson of the morning is now finished and we are able, without disturbing anybody, to visit the mosque.

When we return to the great courtyard, with its battlemented walls, it is the hour of recreation for this crowd of young men in robes and turbans, who now emerge from the shadow of the sanctuary.

Since the early morning they have remained seated on their mats, immersed in study and prayer, amid the confused buzzing of their thousands of voices; and now they scatter themselves about the contiguous Arab quarters until such time as the evening lessons commence. They walk along in little groups, sometimes holding one another's hands like children; most of them carry their heads high and raise their eyes to the heavens, although the sun which greets them outside dazzles them a little with its rays. They seem innumerable, and as they pass show us faces of the most diverse types. They come from all quarters of the world; some from Baghdad, others from Bassorah, from Mossul and even from the interior of Hedjaz. Those from the north have eyes that are bright and clear; and amongst those from Moghreb, from Morocco and the Sahara, are many whose skins are almost black. But the expression of all the faces is alike: something of ecstasy and of aloofness marks them all; the same detachment, a preoccupation with the self-same dream. And in the sky, to which they raise their eyes, the heavens—framed always by the battlements of El-Azhar—are almost white from the excess of light, with a border of tall, red minarets, which seem to be aglow with the reflection of some great fire. And, watching them pass, all these young priests or jurists, at once so different and so alike, we understand better than before how Islam, the old, old Islam, keeps still its cohesion and its power.

The mosque in which they pursue their studies is now almost empty. In its restful twilight there is silence, and the unexpected music of little birds; it is the brooding season and the ceilings of carved wood are full of nests, which nobody disturbs.

A world, this mosque, in which thousands of people could easily find room. Some hundred and fifty marble columns, brought from ancient temples, support the arches of the seven parallel aisles. There is no light save that which comes through the arcade opening into the courtyard, and it is so dark in the aisles at the far end that we wonder again how the faithful can see to read when the sun of Egypt happens to be veiled.

Some score of students, who seem almost lost

in the vast solitude, still remain during the hour
of rest, and are busy sweeping the floor with long
palms made into a kind of broom. These are
the poor students, whose only meal is of dry
bread, and who at night stretch themselves to
sleep on the same mat on which they have sat
studying during the day.

The residence at the university is free to all
the scholars, the cost of their education and
maintenance being provided by pious donations.
But, inasmuch as the bequests are restricted
according to nationality, there is necessarily
inequality in the treatment doled out to the
different students: thus the young men of a given
country may be almost rich, possessing a room
and a good bed; while those of a neighbouring
country must sleep on the ground and have
barely enough to keep body and soul together.
But none of them complain, and they know how
to help one another.[1]

Near to us, one of these needy students is
eating, without any false shame, his midday
meal of dry bread; and he welcomes with a
smile the sparrows and the other little winged
thieves who come to dispute with him the
crumbs of his repast. And farther down, in the
dimly lighted vaults at the end, is one who dis-

[1] The duration of the studies at El-Azhar varies from three
to six years.

dains to eat, or who, maybe, has no bread; who, when his sweeping is done, reseats himself on his mat, and, opening his Koran, commences to read aloud with the customary intonation. His voice, rich and facile, and moderated with discretion, has a charm that is irresistible in the sonorous old mosque, where at this hour the only other sound is the scarcely perceptible twittering of the little broods above, among the dull gold beams of the ceiling. Those who have been familiar with the sanctuaries of Islam know, as well as I, that there is no book so exquisitely rhythmical as that of the Prophet. Even if the sense of the verses escape you, the chanted reading, which forms part of certain of the offices, acts upon you by the simple magic of its sounds, in the same way as the oratorios which draw tears in the churches of Christ. Rising and falling like some sad lullaby, the declamation of this young priest, with his face of visionary, and garb of decent poverty, swells involuntarily, till gradually it seems to fill the seven deserted aisles of El-Azhar.

We stop in spite of ourselves, and listen, in the midst of the silence of midday. And in this so venerable place, where dilapidation and the usury of centuries are revealed on every side—even on the marble columns worn by the constant friction of hands—this voice of gold that rises

alone seems as if it were intoning the last lament
over the death-pang of Old Islam and the end of
time, the elegy, as it were, of the universal death
of faith in the heart of man.

"Science is one religion; prayer is another. Study is better
than worship. Go; seek knowledge everywhere, if needs be,
even into China." *Verses from the Hadith.*

Amongst us Europeans it is commonly ac-
cepted as a proven fact that Islam is merely a
religion of obscurantism, bringing in its train the
stagnation of nations, and hampering them in
that march to the unknown which we call " progress." But such an attitude shows not only an
absolute ignorance of the teaching of the Prophet,
but a blind forgetfulness of the evidence of history. The Islam of the earlier centuries evolved
and progressed with the nations, and the stimulus
it gave to men in the reign of the ancient caliphs
is beyond all question. To impute to it the
present decadence of the Moslem world is altogether too puerile. The truth is that nations
have their day; and to a period of glorious
splendour succeeds a time of lassitude and
slumber. It is a law of nature. And then one
day some danger threatens them, stirs them from
their torpor and they awake.

This immobility of the countries of the Crescent was once dear to me. If the end is to pass
through life with the minimum of suffering, dis-

daining all vain striving, and to die entranced by
radiant hopes, the Orientals are the only wise
men. But now that greedy nations beset them on
all sides their dreaming is no longer possible.
They must awake, alas.

They must awake; and already the awakening
is at hand. Here, in Egypt, where the need is
felt to change so many things, it is proposed, too,
to reform the old university of El-Azhar, one of
the chief centres of Islam. One thinks of it with
a kind of fear, knowing what danger there is in
laying hands upon institutions which have lasted
for a thousand years. Reform, however, has, in
principle, been decided upon. New knowledge,
brought from the West, is penetrating into the
tabernacle of the Fatimites. Has not the Prophet
said: " Go; seek knowledge far and wide, if
needs be even into China "? What will come
of it? Who can tell? But this, at least, is
certain: that in the dazzling hours of noon, or
in the golden hours of evening, when the crowd
of these modernised students spreads itself over
the vast courtyard, overlooked by its countless
minarets, there will no longer be seen in their
eyes the mystic light of to-day; and it will no
longer be the old unshakable faith, nor the lofty
and serene indifference, nor the profound peace,
that these messengers will carry to the ends of
the Mussulman earth. . . .

IN THE TOMBS OF THE APIS

CHAPTER VI

IN THE TOMBS OF THE APIS

THE dwelling places of the Apis, in the grim darkness beneath the Memphite desert, are, as all the world knows, monster coffins of black granite ranged in catacombs, hot and stifling as eternal stoves.

To reach them from the banks of the Nile we have first to traverse the low region which the inundations of the ancient river, regularly repeated since the beginning of time, have rendered propitious to the growth of plants and to the development of men; an hour or two's journey, this evening through forests of date-trees whose beautiful palms temper the light of the March sun, which is now halfveiled in clouds and already declining. In the distance herds are grazing in the cool shade. And we meet fellahs leading back from the field towards the village on the river-bank their little donkeys, laden with sheaves of corn. The air is mild and wholesome under the high tufts of these endless green plumes, which move in the warm wind almost without noise. We seem to be in some happy land, where the pastoral life should be easy, and even a little paradisaical.

77

But beyond, in front of us, quite a different
world is gradually revealed. Its aspect assumes
the importance of a menace from the unknown;
it awes us like an apparition of chaos, of universal
death. . . . It is the desert, the conquering desert, in the midst of which inhabited Egypt,
the green valleys of the Nile, trace merely a
narrow ribbon. And here, more than elsewhere,
the sight of this sovereign desert rising up before
us is startling and thrilling, so high up it seems,
and we so low in the Edenlike valley shaded by
the palms. With its yellow hues, its livid mar-
blings, and its sands which make it look somehow as if it lacked consistency, it rises on the
whole horizon like a kind of soft wall or a great
fearsome cloud—or rather, like a long cataclysmic
wave, which does not move indeed, but which, if
it did, would overwhelm and swallow everything.
It is the *Memphite desert*—a place, that is to
say, such as does not exist elsewhere on earth; a
fabulous necropolis, in which men of earlier times,
heaped up for some three thousand years the
embalmed bodies of their dead, exaggerating, as
time went on, the foolish grandeur of their tombs.
Now, above the sand which looks like the front
of some great tidal wave arrested in its progress,
we see on all sides, and far into the distance,
triangles of superhuman proportions which were
once the tombs of mummies; pyramids, still

upright, all of them, on their sinister pedestal
of sand. Some are comparatively near; others
almost lost in the background of the solitudes
—and perhaps more awesome in that they are
merely outlined in grey, high up among the
clouds.

.   .   .   .

The little carriages that have brought us to the
necropolis of Memphis, through the interminable
forest of palm-trees, had their wheels fitted with
large pattens for their journey over the sand.

Now, arrived at the foot of the fearsome
region, we commence to climb a hill where all
at once the trot of our horses ceases to be heard;
the moving felting of the soil establishes a sudden
silence around us, as indeed is always the case
when we reach these sands. It seems as if it
were a silence of respect which the desert itself
imposes.

The valley of life sinks and fades behind us,
until at last it disappears, hidden by a line of
sandhills—the first wave, as one might say, of
this waterless sea—and we are now mounted into
the kingdom of the dead, swept at this moment
by a withering and almost icy wind, which from
below one would not have expected.

This desert of Memphis has not yet been profaned by hotels or motor roads, such as we have
seen in the " little desert " of the Sphinx—whose

three pyramids indeed we can discern at the extreme limit of the view, prolonging almost to infinity for our eyes this domain of mummies. There is nobody to be seen, nor any indication of the present day, amongst these mournful undulations of yellow or pale grey sand, in which we seem lost as in the swell of an ocean. The sky is cloudy—such as you can scarcely imagine the sky of Egypt. And in this immense nothingness of sand and stones, which stands out now more clearly against the clouds on the horizon, there is nothing anywhere save the silhouettes of those eternal triangles: the pyramids, gigantic things which rise here and there at hazard, some half in ruin, others almost intact and preserving still their sharp point. To-day they are the only landmarks of this necropolis, which is nearly six miles in length, and was formerly covered by temples of a magnificence and a vastness unimaginable to the minds of our day. Except for one which is quite near us (the fantastic grandfather of the others, that of King Zoser, who died nearly 5000 years ago), except for this one, which is made of six colossal superposed terraces, they are all built after that same conception of the *Triangle,* which is at once the most mysteriously simple figure of geometry, and the strongest and most permanently stable form of architecture. And now that there remains no trace of the frescoed portraits which used to adorn them, nor of their multicoloured coatings, now that they have taken on the same dead colour as the desert, they look like the huge bones of giant fossils, that have long outlasted their other con-temporaries on earth.   Beneath the ground, how-ever, the case is different; there, still remain the bodies of men, and even of cats and birds, who with their own eyes saw these vast structures building, and who sleep intact, swathed in band-ages, in the darkness of their tunnels. *We know,* for we have penetrated there before, what things are hidden in the womb of this old desert, on which the yellow shroud of the sand grows thicker and thicker as the centuries pass.   The whole deep rock has been perforated patiently to make hypogea and sepulchral chambers, great and small, and veritable palaces for the dead, adorned with innumerable painted figures.   And though now, for some two thousand years, men have set themselves furiously to exhume the sarcophagi and the treasures that are buried here, the subterranean reserves are not yet exhausted. There still remain, no doubt, pleiads of undis-turbed sleepers, who will never be discovered.

As we advance the wind grows stronger and colder beneath a sky that becomes increasingly cloudy, and the sand is flying on all sides.   The sand is the undisputed sovereign of this necropolis; if it does not surge and roll like some enormous tidal wave, as it appears to do when seen from the green valley below, it nevertheless covers everything with an obstinate persistence which has continued since the beginning of time. Already at Memphis it has buried innumerable statues and colossi and temples of the Sphinx. It comes without a pause, from Libya, from the Great Sahara, which contain enough to powder the universe. It harmonises well with the tall skeletons of the pyramids, which form immutable rocks on its always shifting extent; and if one thinks of it, it gives a more thrilling sense of anterior eternities even than all these Egyptian ruins, which, in comparison with it, are things of yesterday. The sand—the sand of the primitive seas—which represents a labour of erosion of a duration impossible to conceive, and bears witness to a continuity of destruction which, one might say, had no beginning.

Here, in the midst of these solitudes, is a humble habitation, old and half buried in sand, at which we have to stop. It was once the house of the Egyptologist Mariette, and still shelters the director of the excavations, from whom we have to obtain permission to descend amongst the Apis. The whitewashed room in which he receives us is encumbered with the age-old debris which he is continually bringing to light. The parting rays of the sun, which shines low down from between two clouds, enter through a window opening on to the surrounding desolation; and the light comes mournfully, yellowed by the sand and the evening.

The master of the house, while his Bedouin servants are gone to open and light up for us the underground habitations of the Apis, shows us his latest astonishing find, made this morning in a hypogeum of one of the most ancient dynasties. It is there on a table, a group of little people of wood, of the size of the marionettes of our theatres. And since it was the custom to put in a tomb only those figures or objects which were most pleasing to him who dwelt in it, the man-mummy to whom this toy was offered in times anterior to all precise chronology must have been extremely partial to dancing-girls. In the middle of the group the man himself is represented, sitting in an armchair, and on his knee he holds his favourite dancing-girl. Other girls posture before him in a dance of the period; and on the ground sit musicians touching tambourines and strangely fashioned harps. All wear their hair in a long plait, which falls below their shoulders like the pigtail of the Chinese. It was the distinguishing mark of these kinds of courtesans. And these little people had kept their pose in the darkness for some three thousand years before the commencement of the Christian era. . . . In order to show it to us better the group is brought to the window, and the mournful light which enters from across the infinite solitudes of the desert colours them yellow and shows us in detail their little doll-like attitudes and their comical and frightened appearance—frightened perhaps to find themselves so old and issuing from so deep a night. They had not seen a setting of the sun, such as they now regard with their queer eyes, too long and too wide open, they had not seen such a thing for some five thousand years. . . .

The habitation of the Apis, the lords of the necropolis, is little more than two hundred yards away. We are told that the place is now lighted up and that we may betake ourselves thither.

The descent is by a narrow, rapidly sloping passage, dug in the soil, between banks of sand and broken stones. We are now completely sheltered from the bitter wind which blows across the desert, and from the dark doorway that opens before us comes a breath of air as from an oven. It is always dry and hot in the underground funeral places of Egypt, which make indeed admirable stoves for mummies. The threshold once crossed we are plunged first of all in darkness and, preceded by a lantern, make our way, by devious turnings, over large flagstones, passing obelisks, fallen blocks of stone and other gigantic debris, in a heat that continually increases.

At last the principal artery of the hypogeum appears, a thoroughfare more than five hundred yards long, cut in the rock, where the Bedouins have prepared for us the customary feeble light.

It is a place of fearful aspect. As soon as one enters one is seized by the sense of a mournfulness beyond words, by an oppression as of something too heavy, too crushing, almost superhuman. The impotent little flames of the candles, placed in a row, in groups of fifty, on tripods of wood from one end of the route to the other, show on the right and left of the immense avenue rectangular sepulchral caverns, containing each a black coffin, but a coffin as if for a mastodon. And all these coffins, so sombre and so alike, are square shaped too, severely simple like so many boxes; but made out of a single block of rare granite that gleams like marble. They are entirely without ornament. It is necessary to look closely to distinguish on the smooth walls the hieroglyphic inscriptions, the rows of little figures, little owls, little jackals, that tell in a lost language the history of ancient peoples. Here is the signature of King Amasis; beyond, that of King Cam-

byses. . . . Who were the Titans who, century
after century, were able to hew these coffins (they
are at least twelve feet long by ten feet high),
and, having hewn them, to carry them underground (they weigh on an average between sixty
and seventy tons), and finally to range them in
rows here in these strange chambers, where they
stand as if in ambuscade on either side of us as we
pass? Each in its turn has contained quite com-
fortably the mummy of a bull Apis, armoured in
plates of gold. But in spite of their weight, in
spite of their solidity which effectively defies
destruction, they have been despoiled [1]—when is
not precisely known, probably by the soldiers of
the King of Persia. And this notwithstanding
that merely to open them represents a labour
of astonishing strength and patience. In some
cases the thieves have succeeded, by the aid of
levers, in moving a few inches the formidable
lid; in others, by persevering with blows of
pickaxes, they have pierced, in the thickness of
the granite, a hole through which a man has been
enabled to crawl like a rat, or a worm, and

---

[1] One, however, remains intact in its walled cavern, and
thus preserves for us the only Apis which has come down to
our days. And one recalls the emotion of Mariette, when, on
entering it, he saw on the sandy ground the imprint of the
naked feet of the last Egyptian who left it thirty-seven centuries before.

then, groping his way, to plunder the sacred mummy.

What strikes us most of all in the colossal hypogeum is the meeting there, in the middle of the stairway by which we leave, with yet another black coffin, which lies across our path as if to bar it. It is as monstrous and as simple as the others, its seniors, which many centuries before, as the deified bulls died, had commenced to line the great straight thoroughfare. But this one has never reached its place and never held its mummy. It was the last. Even while men were slowly rolling it, with tense muscles and panting cries, towards what might well have seemed its eternal chamber, other gods were born, and the cult of the Apis had come to an end—suddenly, then and there! Such a fate may happen indeed to each and all of the religions and institutions of men, even to those most deeply rooted in their hearts and their ancestral past. . . . That perhaps is the most disturbing of all our positive notions: to know that there will be a *last* of all things, not only a last temple, and a last priest, but a last birth of a human child, a last sunrise, a last day. . . .

.   .   .   .

In these hot catacombs we had forgotten the cold wind that blew outside, and the physiognomy of the Memphite desert, the aspects of horror that were awaiting us above had vanished from our mind. Sinister as it is under a blue sky, this desert becomes absolutely intolerable to look upon if by chance the sky is cloudy when the daylight fails.

On our return to it, from the subterranean darkness, everything in its dead immensity has begun to take on the blue tint of the night. On the top of the sandhills, of which the yellow colour has greatly paled since we went below, the wind amuses itself by raising little vortices of sand that imitate the spray of an angry sea. On all sides dark clouds stretch themselves as at the moment of our descent. The horizon detaches itself more and more clearly from them, and, farther towards the east, it actually seems to be tilted up; one of the highest of the waves of this waterless sea, a mountain of sand whose soft contours are deceptive in the distance, makes it look as if it sloped towards us, so as almost to produce a sensation of vertigo. The sun itself has deigned to remain on the scene a few seconds longer, held beyond its time by the effect of mirage; but it is so changed behind its thick veils that we would prefer that it should not be there. Of the colour of dying embers, it seems too near and too large; it has ceased to give any light, and is become a mere rose-coloured globe, that is losing its shape and becoming oval. No longer in the free heavens, but stranded there on the extreme edge of the desert, it watches the scene like a large dull eye, about to close itself in death. And the mysterious superhuman triangles, they too, of course, are there, waiting for us on our return from underground, some near, some far, posted in their eternal places; but surely they have grown larger in the twilight, which grows gradually more blue. . . .

Such a night, in such a place, it seems the *last* night.

THE OUTSKIRTS
OF CAIRO

CHAPTER VII

NIGHT. A long straight road, the artery of some capital, through which our carriage drives at a fast trot, making a deafening clatter on the pavement. Electric light everywhere. The shops are closing; it must needs be late.

The road is Levantine in its general character: and we should have no clear notion of the place did we not see in our rapid, noisy passage signs that recall us to the land of the Arabs. People pass dressed in the long robe and tarboosh of the East; and some of the houses, above the European shops, are ornamented with mushrabiyas. But this blinding electricity strikes a false note. In our hearts are we quite sure we are in the East?

The road ends, opening on to darkness. Suddenly, without any warning, it abuts upon a void in which the eyes see nothing, and we roll over a yielding, felted soil, where all noise abruptly ceases—it is the *desert!* . . . Not a vague, nondescript stretch of country such as in the outskirts of our towns, not one of the solitudes of Europe, but the threshold of the vast desolations of Arabia. *The desert;* and, even if we had not known that it was awaiting us, we should have recognised it by its indescribable quality of harshness and uniqueness which, in spite of the darkness, cannot be mistaken.

But the night after all is not so black. It only seemed so, at the first moment, by contrast with the glaring illumination of the street. In reality it is transparent and blue. A half-moon, high up in the heavens, and veiled by a diaphanous mist, shines gently, and as it is an Egyptian moon, more subtle than ours, it leaves to things a little of their colour. We can see now, as well as feel, this desert, which has opened and imposed its silence upon us. Before us is the paleness of its sands and the reddish-brown of its dead rocks. Verily, in no country but Egypt are there such rapid surprises: to issue from a street flanked by shops and stalls and, without transition, to find this! . . .

Our horses have, inevitably, to slacken speed as the wheels of our carriage sink into the sand. Around us still are some stray ramblers, who presently assume the air of ghosts, with their long black or white draperies, and noiseless tread. And then, not a soul; nothing but the sand and the moon.

But now almost at once, after the short inter-

vening nothingness, we find ourselves in a
new town; streets with little low houses, little
cross-roads, little squares, all of them white, on
whitened sands, beneath a white moon. . . .
But there is no electricity in this town, no
lights, and nobody is stirring; doors and windows
are shut: no movement of any kind, and the
silence, at first, is like that of the surrounding
desert. It is a town in which the half-light of
the moon, amongst so much vague whiteness,
is diffused in such a way that it seems to come
from all sides at once and things cast no shadows
which might give them definiteness; a town
where the soil is so yielding that our progress is
weakened and retarded, as in dreams. It seems
unreal: and, in penetrating farther into it, a
sense of fear comes over you that can neither
be dismissed nor defined.

For assuredly this is no ordinary town. . . .
And yet the houses, with their windows barred
like those of a harem, are in no way singular—
except that they are shut and silent. It is all
this whiteness, perhaps, which freezes us. And
then, too, the silence is not, in fact, like that of
the desert, which did at least seem natural,
inasmuch as there was nothing there; here, on
the contrary, there is a sense of innumerable
presences, which shrink away as you pass but
nevertheless continue to watch attentively. . . .

We pass mosques in total darkness and they too are silent and white, with a slight bluish tint cast on them by the moon. And sometimes, between the houses, there are little enclosed spaces, like narrow gardens, but which can have no possible verdure. And in these gardens numbers of little obelisks rise from the sand— white obelisks, it is needless to say, for to-night we are in the kingdom of absolute whiteness. What can they be, these strange little gardens? . . . And the sand, meanwhile, which covers the streets with its thick coatings, continues to deaden the sound of our progress, out of compliment no doubt to all these watchful things that are so silent around us.

At the crossings and in the little squares the obelisks become more numerous, erected always at either end of a slab of stone that is about the length of a man. Their little motionless groups, posted as if on the watch, seem so little real in their vague whiteness that we feel tempted to verify them by touching, and, verily, we should not be astonished if our hand passed through them as through a ghost. Farther on there is a wide expanse without any houses at all, where these ubiquitous little obelisks abound in the sand like ears of corn in a field. There is now no further room for illusion. We are in a cemetery, and have been passing in the midst of

houses of the dead, and mosques of the dead, in
a town of the dead.

Once emerged from this cemetery, which in
the end at least disclosed itself in its true character, we are involved again in the continuation
of the mysterious town, which takes us back
into its network. Little houses follow one another as before, only now the little gardens are
replaced by little burial enclosures. And everything grows more and more indistinct, in the
gentle light, which gradually grows less. It is
as if someone were putting frosted globes over
the moon, so that soon, but for the transparency
of this air of Egypt and the prevailing whiteness
of things, there would be no light at all. Once
at a window the light of a lamp appears; it is
the lantern of gravediggers. Anon we hear the
voices of men chanting a prayer; and the prayer
is a prayer for the dead.

These tenantless houses were never built for
dwellings. They are simply places where men
assemble on certain anniversaries, to pray for the
dead. Every Moslem family of any note has its
little temple of this kind, near to the family
graves. And there are so many of them that
now the place is become a town—and a town in
the desert—that is to say, in a place useless for
any other purpose; a secure place indeed, for we
may be sure that the ground occupied by these

poor tombs runs no risk of being coveted—not
even in the irreverent times of the future. No,
it is on the other side of Cairo—on the other
bank of the Nile, amongst the verdure of the
palm-trees, that we must look for the suburb in
course of transformation, with its villas of the
invading foreigner, and the myriad electric lights
along its motor roads. On this side there is no
such fear; the peace and desuetude are eternal;
and the winding sheet of the Arabian sands is
ready always for its burial office.

At the end of this town of the dead, the desert
again opens before us its mournful whitened
expanse. On such a night as this, when the
wind blows cold and the misty moon shows like
a sad opal, it looks like a steppe under snow.

But it is a desert planted with ruins, with the
ghosts of mosques; a whole colony of high
tumbling domes are scattered here at hazard
on the shifting extent of the sands. And what
strange old-fashioned domes they are! The
archaism of their silhouettes strikes us from the
first, as much as their isolation in such a place.
They look like bells, or gigantic dervish hats
placed on pedestals, and those farthest away
give the impression of squat, large-headed figures
posted there as sentinels, watching the vague
horizon of Arabia beyond.

They are the proud tombs of the fourteenth

and fifteenth centuries where the Mameluke Sultans, who oppressed Egypt for nearly three hundred years, sleep now in complete abandonment. Nowadays, it is true, some visits are beginning to be paid to them—on winter nights when the moon is full and they throw on the sands their great clear-cut shadows. At such times the light is considered favourable, and they rank among the curiosities exploited by the agencies. Numbers of tourists (who persist in calling them the tombs of the caliphs) betake themselves thither of an evening—a noisy caravan mounted on little donkeys. But to-night the moon is too pale and uncertain, and we shall no doubt be alone in troubling them in their ghostly communion.

To-night indeed the light is quite unusual. As just now in the town of the dead, it is diffused on all sides and gives even to the most massive objects the transparent semblance of unreality. But nevertheless it shows their detail and leaves them something of their daylight colouring, so that all these funeral domes, raised on the ruins of the mosques, which serve them as pedestals, have preserved their reddish or brown colours, although the sand which separates them, and makes between the tombs of the different sultans little dead solitudes, remains pale and wan.

And meanwhile our carriage, proceeding always without noise, traces on this same sand little furrows which the wind will have effaced by to-morrow. There are no roads of any kind; they would indeed be as useless as they are impossible to make. You may pass here where you list, and fancy yourself far away from any place inhabited by living beings. The great town, which we know to be so close, appears from time to time, thanks to the undulations of the ground, as a mere phosphorescence, a reflection of its myriad electric lights. We are indeed in the desert of the dead, in the sole company of the moon, which, by the fantasy of this wonderful Egyptian sky, is to-night a moon of grey pearl, one might almost say a moon of mother-of-pearl.

Each of these funeral mosques is a thing of splendour, if one examines it closely in its solitude. Those strange upraised domes, which from a distance look like the head-dresses of dervishes or magi, are embroidered with arabesques, and the walls are crowned with denticulated trefoils of exquisite fashioning.

But nobody venerates these tombs of the Mameluke oppressors, or keeps them in repair; and within them there are no more chants, no prayers to Allah. Night after night they pass in an infinity of silence. Piety contents itself with not destroying them; leaving them there at the mercy of time and the sun and the wind which

withers and crumbles them.   And all around are
the signs of ruin.   Tottering cupolas show us
irreparable cracks; the halves of broken arches
are outlined to-night in shadow against the
mother-of-pearl light of the sky, and debris of
sculptured stones are strewn about.   But nevertheless these tombs, that are well-nigh accursed,
still stir in us a vague sense of alarm—particularly those in the distance, which rise up like silhouettes of misshapen giants in enormous hats—
dark on the white sheet of sand—and stand there
in groups, or scattered in confusion, at the entrance to the vast empty regions beyond.

.   .   .   .

We had chosen a time when the light was
doubtful in order that we might avoid the
tourists, but as we approach the funeral dwelling of Sultan Barkuk, the assassin, we see, issuing from it, a whole band, some twenty in a line,
who emerge from the darkness of the abandoned
walls, each trotting on his little donkey and each
followed by the inevitable Bedouin driver, who
taps with his stick upon the rump of the beast.
They are returning to Cairo, their visit ended,
and exchange in a loud voice, from one ass to
another, more or less inept impressions in various
European languages. . . . And look! there is
even amongst them the almost proverbial belated
dame who, for private reasons of her own, follows

at a respectable distance behind. She is a little mature perhaps, so far as can be judged in the moonlight, but nevertheless still sympathetic to her driver, who, with both hands, supports her from behind on her saddle, with a touching solicitude that is peculiar to the country. Ah! these little donkeys of Egypt, so observant, so philosophical and sly, why cannot they write their memoirs! What a number of droll things they must have seen at night in the outskirts of Cairo!

This good lady evidently belongs to that extensive category of hardy explorers who, despite their high respectability at home, do not hesitate, once they are landed on the banks of the Nile, to supplement their treatment by the sun and the dry winds with a little of the " Bedouin cure."

ARCHAIC CHRISTIANITY

CHAPTER VIII

DIMLY lighted by the flames of a few poor
slender tapers which flicker against the walls in
stone niches, a dense crowd of human figures
veiled in black, in a place overpowering and suffocating—underground, no doubt—which is filled
with the perfume of the incense of Arabia: and a
noise of almost wicked movement, which stirs us
to alarm and even horror: bleatings of new-born
babies, cries of distress of tiny mites whose
voices are drowned, as if on purpose, by a
clinking of cymbals. . . .

What can it be? Why have they descended
into this dark hole, these little ones, who howl
in the midst of the smoke, held by these phantoms
in mourning? Had we entered it unawares we
might have thought it a den of wicked sorcery,
an underground cavern for the black mass.

But no. It is the crypt of the basilica of
St Sergius during the Coptic mass of Easter
morning. And when, after the first surprise,
we examine these phantoms, we find that, for
the most part, they are young mothers, with the
refined and gentle faces of Madonnas, who hold

the plaintive little ones beneath their black veils
and seek to comfort them. And the sorcerer,
who plays the cymbals, is a kind old priest, or
sacristan, who smiles paternally. If he makes
all this noise, in a rhythm which in itself is full
of joy, it is to mark the gladness of Easter morn,
to celebrate the resurrection of Christ—and a
little, too, no doubt, to distract the little ones,
some of whom are woefully put out. But their
mammas do not prolong the proof—a mere
momentary visit to this venerable place, which
is to bring them happiness, and they carry their
babes away: and others are led in by the dark,
narrow staircase, so low that one cannot stand
upright in it. And thus the crypt is not
emptied. And meanwhile mass is being said
in the Church overhead.

But what a number of people, of black veils,
are in this hovel, where the air can scarcely be
breathed, and where the barbarous music, mingled with wailings and cries, deafens you! And
what an air of antiquity marks all things here!
The defaced walls, the low roof that one can
easily touch, the granite pillars which sustain the
shapeless arches, are all blackened by the smoke
of the wax candles, and scarred and worn by the
friction of human hands.

At the end of the crypt there is a very sacred
recess round which a crowd presses: a coarse

niche, a little larger than those cut in the wall
to receive the tapers, a niche which covers the
ancient stone on which, according to tradition,
the Virgin Mary rested, with the child Jesus, in
the course of the flight into Egypt. This holy
stone is sadly worn to-day and polished smooth
by the touch of many pious hands, and the
Byzantine cross which once was carved on it is
almost effaced.

But even if the Virgin had never rested there,
the humble crypt of St Sergius would remain
no less one of the oldest Christian sanctuaries in
the world. And the Copts who still assemble
there with veneration have preceded by many
years the greater part of our Western nations in
the religion of the Bible.

Although the history of Egypt envelops itself
in a sort of night at the moment of the appearance of Christianity, we know that the growth
of the new faith there was as rapid and impetuous as the germination of plants under the
overflow of the Nile. The old Pharaonic cults,
amalgamated at that time with those of Greece,
were so obscured under a mass of rites and formulæ, that they had ceased to have any mean-
ing. And nevertheless here, as in imperial Rome,
there brooded the ferment of a passionate mysti-
cism. Moreover, this Egyptian people, more
than any other, was haunted by the terror of

death, as is proved by the folly of its embalm-
ments.   With what avidity therefore must it
have received the Word of fraternal love and
immediate resurrection.

In any case Christianity was so firmly im-
planted in this Egypt that centuries of persecu-
tion did not succeed in destroying it.   As one
goes up the Nile, many little human settlements
are to be seen, little groups of houses of dried
mud, where the whitened dome of the modest
house of prayer is surmounted by a cross and
not a crescent.   They are the villages of those
Copts, those Egyptians, who have preserved the
Christian faith from father to son since the
nebulous times of the first martyrs.

.   .   .   .

The simple Church of St Sergius is a relic
hidden away and almost buried in the midst of a
labyrinth of ruins.   Without a guide it is almost
impossible to find your way thither.   The quarter
in which it is situated is enclosed within the walls
of what was once a Roman fortress, and this
fortress in its turn is surrounded by the tranquil
ruins of " Old Cairo "—which is to the Cairo
of the Mamelukes and the Khedives, in a small
degree, what Versailles is to Paris.

On this Easter morning, having set out from
the Cairo of to-day to be present at this mass,
we have first to traverse a suburb in course of

transformation, upon whose ancient soil will
shortly appear numbers of those modern horrors,
in mud and metal—factories or large hotels—
which multiply in this poor land with a stupefying rapidity. Then comes a mile or so of uncultivated ground, mixed with stretches of sand,
and already a little desertlike. And then the
walls of Old Cairo; after which begins the peace
of the deserted houses, of little gardens and or-
chards among the ruins. The wind and the dust
beset us the whole way, the almost eternal wind
and the eternal dust of this land, by which, since
the beginning of the ages, so many human eyes
have been burnt beyond recovery. They keep
us now in blinding whirlwinds, which swarm
with flies. The " season " indeed is already over,
and the foreign invaders have fled until next
autumn. Egypt is now more Egyptian, beneath
a more burning sky. The sun of this Easter
Sunday is as hot as ours of July, and the ground
seems as if it would perish of drought. But it
is always thus in the springtime of this rainless
country; the trees, which have kept their leaves
throughout the winter, shed them in April as ours
do in November. There is no shade anywhere
and everything suffers. Everything grows yellow on the yellow sands. But there is no cause
for uneasiness: the inundation is at hand, which
has never failed since the commencement of our

geological period.   In another few weeks the
prodigious river will spread along its banks, just
as in the times of the God Amen, a precocious
and impetuous life.   And meanwhile the orange-
trees, the jasmine and the honeysuckle, which
men have taken care to water with water from the
Nile, are full of riotous bloom.   As we pass the
gardens of Old Cairo, which alternate with the
tumbling houses, this continual cloud of white
dust that envelops us comes suddenly laden with
their sweet fragrance; so that, despite the drought
and the bareness of the trees, the scents of a sudden and feverish springtime are already in the air.

When we arrive at the walls of what used to
be the Roman citadel we have to descend from
our carriage, and passing through a low doorway
penetrate on foot into the labyrinth of a Coptic
quarter which is dying of dust and old age.
Deserted houses that have become the refuges
of outcasts; mushrabiyas, worm-eaten and de-
cayed; little mousetrap alleys that lead us under
arches of the Middle Ages, and sometimes
close over our heads by reason of the fantastic
bending of the ruins.   Even by such a route as
this are we conducted to a famous basilica!
Were it not for these groups of Copts, dressed
in their Sunday garb, who make their way like
us through the ruins to the Easter mass, we
should think that we had lost our way.

And how pretty they look, these women draped like phantoms in their black silks. Their long veils do not completely hide them, as do those of the Moslems. They are simply placed over their hair and leave uncovered the delicate features, the golden necklet and the half-bared arms that carry on their wrists thick twisted bracelets of virgin gold. Pure Egyptians as they are, they have preserved the same delicate profile, the same elongated eyes, as mark the old goddesses carved in bas-relief on the Pharaonic walls. But some, alas, amongst the young ones have discarded their traditional costume, and are arrayed *à la franque,* in gowns and hats. And such gowns, such hats, such flowers! The very peasants of our meanest villages would disdain them. Oh! why cannot someone tell these poor little women, who have it in their power to be so adorable, that the beautiful folds of their black veils give to them an exquisite and characteristic distinction, while this poor tinsel, which recalls the mid-Lent carnivals, makes of them objects that excite our pity!

In one of the walls which now surround us there is a low and shrinking doorway. Can this be the entrance to the basilica? The idea seems absurd. And yet some of the pretty creatures in the black veils and bracelets of gold, who were in front of us, have disappeared through it, and

already the perfume of the censers is wafted towards us. A kind of corridor, astonishingly poor
and old, twists itself suspiciously, and then issues
into a narrow court, more than a thousand years
old, where offertory boxes, fixed on Oriental
brackets, invite our alms. The odour of the incense becomes more pronounced, and at last a
door, hidden in shadow at the end of this retreat,
gives access to the venerable church itself.

The church! It is a mixture of Byzantine
basilica, mosque and desert hut. Entering there,
it is as if we were introduced suddenly to the
naive infancy of Christianity, as if we surprised
it, as it were, in its cradle—which was indeed
Oriental. The triple nave is full of little children (here also, that is what strikes us first),
of little mites who cry or else laugh and play;
and there are mothers suckling their new-born
babes—and all the time the invisible mass is
being celebrated beyond, behind the iconostasis.
On the ground, on mats, whole families are
seated in circle, as if they were in their homes.
A thick deposit of white chalk on the defaced,
shrunken walls bears witness to great age. And
over all this is a strange old ceiling of cedarwood,
traversed by large barbaric beams.

In the nave, supported by columns of marble,
brought in days gone by from Pagan temples,
there are, as in all these old Coptic churches,

high transverse wooden partitions, elaborately
wrought in the Arab fashion, which divide it
into three sections: the first, into which one
comes on entering the church, is allotted to the
women, the second is for the baptistery, and
the third, at the end adjoining the iconostasis,
is reserved for the men.

These women who are gathered this morning
in their apportioned space—so much at home
there with their suckling little ones—wear, almost all of them, the long black silk veils of
former days. In their harmonious and endlessly
restless groups, the gowns *à la franque* and the
poor hats of carnival are still the exception.
The congregation, as a whole, preserves almost
intact its naive, old-time favour.

And there is movement too, beyond, in the
compartment of the men, which is bounded at
the farther end by the iconostasis—a thousand-
year-old wall decorated with inlaid cedarwood
and ivory of precious antique workmanship, and
adorned with strange old icons, blackened by
time. It is behind this wall—pierced by several
doorways—that mass is now being said. From
this last sanctuary shut off thus from the people
comes the vague sound of singing; from time to
time a priest raises a faded silk curtain and from
the threshold makes the sign of blessing. His
vestments are of gold, and he wears a golden

crown, but the humble faithful speak to him
freely, and even touch his gorgeous garments,
that might be those of one of the Wise Kings.
He smiles, and letting fall the curtain, which
covers the entrance to the tabernacle, disappears
again into his innocent mystery.

Even the least things here tell of decay. The
flagstones, trodden by the feet of numberless
dead generations, are become uneven through the
settling of the soil. Everything is askew, bent,
dusty and worn-out. The daylight comes from
above, through narrow barred windows. There
is a lack of air, so that one almost stifles. But
though the sun does not enter, a certain in-
definable reflection from the whitened walls re-
minds us that outside there is a flaming, resplendent Eastern spring.

In this, the old grandfather, as it were, of
churches, filled now with a cloud of odorous
smoke, what one hears, more even than the
chanting of the mass, is the ceaseless movement,
the pious agitation of the faithful; and more
even than that, the startling noise that rises
from the holy crypt below—the sharp clashing
of cymbals and those multitudinous little wailings, that sound like the mewings of kittens.

But let me not harbour thoughts of irony!
Surely not. If, in our Western lands, certain
ceremonies seem to me anti-Christian—as, for

example, one of those spectacular high masses in the over-pompous Cathedral of Cologne, where halberdiers overawe the crowd—here, on the contrary, the simplicity of this primitive cult is touching and respectable in the extreme. These Copts who instal themselves in their church as round their firesides, who make their home there and encumber the place with their fretful little ones, have, in their own way, well understood the words of Him who said: " Suffer the little children to come unto Me, and do not forbid them, for of such is the kingdom of God."

THE RACE OF BRONZE

CHAPTER IX

A MONOTONOUS chant on three notes, which must
date from the first Pharaohs, may still be heard
in our days on the banks of the Nile, from the
Delta as far as Nubia. At different places along
the river, half-nude men, with torsos of bronze
and voices all alike, intone it in the morning when
they commence their endless labours and continue it throughout the day, until the evening
brings repose.

Whoever has journeyed in a dahabiya up the
old river will remember this song of the water-
drawers, with its accompaniment, in slow cadence,
of creakings of wet wood.

It is the song of the " shadûf," and the
" shadûf " is a primitive rigging, which has remained unchanged since times beyond all reckon-
ing. It is composed of a long antenna, like the
yard of a tartan, which is supported in see-saw
fashion on an upright beam, and carries at its
extremity a wooden bucket. A man, with
movements of singular beauty, works it while
he sings, lowers the antenna, draws the water
from the river, and raises the filled bucket, which

another man catches in its ascent and empties
into a basin made out of the mud of the river
bank. When the river is low there are three
such basins, placed one above the other, as if
they were stages by which the precious water
mounts to the fields of corn and lucerne. And
then three " shadûfs," one above the other, creak
together, lowering and raising their great scara-
bæus' horns to the rhythm of the same song.

All along the banks of the Nile this movement
of the antennæ of the shadûfs is to be seen. It
had its beginning in the earliest ages and is still
the characteristic manifestation of human life
along the river banks. It ceases only in the
summer, when the river, swollen by the rains of
equatorial Africa, overflows this land of Egypt,
which it itself has made in the midst of the
Saharan sands. But in the winter, which is here
a time of luminous drought and changeless blue
skies, it is in full swing. Then every day, from
dawn until the evening prayer, the men are busy
at their water-drawing, transformed for the time
into tireless machines, with muscles that work
like metal bands. The action never changes,
any more than the song, and often their thoughts
must wander from their automatic toil, and lose
themselves in some dream, akin to that of their
ancestors who were yoked to the same rigging
four or five thousand years ago. Their torsos,

deluged at each rising of the overflowing bucket, stream constantly with cold water; and sometimes the wind is icy, even while the sun burns; but these perpetual workers are, as we have said, of bronze, and their hardened bodies take no harm.

These men are the fellahs, the peasants of the valley of the Nile—pure Egyptians, whose type has not changed in the course of centuries. In the oldest of the bas-reliefs of Thebes or Memphis you may see many such, with the same noble profile and thickish lips, the same elongated eyes shadowed by heavy eyelids, the same slender figure, surmounted by broad shoulders.

The women who from time to time descend to the river, to draw water also, but in their case in the vases of potters' clay which they carry—this fetching and carrying of the life-giving water is the one primordial occupation in this Egypt, which has no rain, nor any living spring, and subsists only by its river—these women walk and posture with an inimitable grace, draped in black veils, which even the poorest allow to trail behind them, like the train of a court dress. In this bright land, with its rose-coloured distances, it is strange to see them, all so sombrely clothed, spots of mourning, as it were, in the gay fields and the flaring desert. Machine-like creatures, all untaught, they yet possess by instinct, as did once the daughters of Hellas, a sense of nobility in attitude and carriage. None of the women of Europe could wear these coarse black stuffs with such a majestic harmony, and none surely could so raise their bare arms to place on their heads the heavy jars filled with Nile water, and then, departing, carry themselves so proudly, so upright and resilient under their burden.

The muslin tunics which they wear are invariably black like the veils, set off perhaps with some red embroidery or silver spangles. They are unfastened across the chest, and, by a narrow opening which descends to the girdle, disclose the amber-coloured flesh, the median swell of bosoms of pale bronze, which, during their ephemeral youth at least, are of a perfect contour. The faces, it is true, when they are not hidden from you by a fold of the veil, are generally disappointing. The rude labours, the early maternity and lactations, soon age and wither them. But if by chance you see a young woman she is usually an apparition of beauty, at once vigorous and slender.

As for the fellah babies, who abound in great numbers and follow, half naked, their mammas or their big sisters, they would for the most part be adorable little creatures, were it not for the dirtiness which in this country is a thing almost prescribed by tradition. Round their eyelids and their moist lips are glued little clusters of Egyptian flies, which are considered here to be beneficial to the children, and the latter have no thought of driving them away, so resigned are they become, by force of heredity, to whatever annoyance they thereby suffer. Another example indeed of the passivity which their fathers show when brought face to face with the invading foreigners!

Passivity and meek endurance seem to be the characteristics of this inoffensive people, so graceful in their rags, so mysterious in their age-old immobility, and so ready to accept with an equal indifference whatever yoke may come. Poor, beautiful people, with muscles that never grow tired! Whose men in olden times moved the great stones of the temples, and knew no burden that was too heavy; whose women, with their slender, pale-tawny arms and delicate small hands, surpass by far in strength the burliest of our peasants! Poor beautiful race of bronze! No doubt it was too precocious and put forth too soon its astonishing flower—in times when the other peoples of the earth were still vegetating in obscurity; no doubt its present resignation comes from lassitude, after so many centuries of effort and expansive power. Once it monopolised the glory of the world, and here it is

now—for some two thousand years—fallen into
a kind of tired sleep, which has left it an easy
prey alike to the conquerors of yesterday and
to the exploiters of to-day.

Another trait which, side by side with their
patience, prevails amongst these true-blooded
Egyptians of the countryside is their attachment
to the soil, to the soil which nourishes them, and
in which later on they will sleep. To possess
land, to forestall at any price the smallest portion of it, to reclaim patches of it from the
shifting desert, that is the sole aim, or almost
so, which the fellahs pursue in this world: to
possess a field, however small it may be—a field,
moreover, which they till with the oldest plough
invented by man, the exact design of which may
be seen carved on the walls of the tombs at
Memphis.

And this same people, which was the first of
any to conceive magnificence, whose gods and
kings were formerly surrounded with an overpowering splendour, contrives to live to-day,
pell-mell with its sheep and goats, in humble,
low-roofed cabins made out of sunbaked mud!
The Egyptian villages are all of the neutral
colour of the soil; a little white chalk brightens,
perhaps, the minaret or cupola of the mosque;
but except for that little refuge, whither folk
come to pray each evening—for no one here

would retire for the night without having first
prostrated himself before the majesty of Allah
—everything is of a mournful grey. Even the
costumes of the people are dull-coloured and
wretched-looking. It is an East grown poor
and old, although the sky remains as wonderful
as ever.

But all this past grandeur has left its imprint
on the fellahs. They have a refinement of appearance and manner, all unknown amongst
the majority of the good people of our villages.
And those amongst them who by good fortune
become prosperous have forthwith a kind of distinction, and seem to know, as if by birth, how
to dispense the gracious hospitality of an aris-
tocrat. The hospitality of even the humblest
preserves something of courtesy and ease, which
tells of breed. I remember those clear evenings
when, after the peaceful navigation of the day,
I used to stop and draw up my dahabiya to
the bank of the river. (I speak now of out-of-
the-way places—free as yet from the canker
of the tourist element—such as I habitually
chose.) It was in the twilight at the hour when
the stars began to shine out from the golden
green sky. As soon as I put foot upon the
shore, and my arrival was signalled by the bark-
ing of the watchdogs, the chief of the nearest
hamlet always came to meet me. A dignified

man, in a long robe of striped silk or modest blue cotton, he accosted me with formulæ of welcome quite in the grand manner; insisted on my following him to his house of dried mud; and there, escorting me, after the exchange of further compliments, to the place of honour on the poor divan of his lodging, forced me to accept the traditional cup of Arab coffee.

.   .   .   .

To wake these fellahs from their strange sleep, to open their eyes at last, and to transform them by a modern education—that is the task which nowadays a select band of Egyptian patriots is desirous of attempting. Not long ago, such an endeavour would have seemed to me a crime; for these stubborn peasants were living under conditions of the least suffering, rich in faith and poor in desire. But to-day they are suffering from an invasion more undermining, more dangerous than that of the conquerors who killed by sword and fire. The Occidentals are there, everywhere, amongst them, profiting by their meek passivity to turn them into slaves for their business and their pleasure. The work of degradation of these simpletons is so easy: men bring them new desires, new greeds, new needs,—and rob them of their prayers.

Yes, it is time perhaps to wake them from their sleep of more than twenty centuries, to put them on their guard, and to see what yet they may be capable of, what surprises they may have in store for us after that long lethargy, which must surely have been restorative. In any case the human species, in course of deterioration through overstrain, would find amongst these singers of the shadûf and these labourers with the antiquated plough, brains unclouded by alcohol, and a whole reserve of tranquil beauty, of well-balanced physique, of vigour untainted by bestiality.

A CHARMING LUNCHEON

CHAPTER X

WE are making our way through the fields of
Abydos in the dazzling splendour of the forenoon,
having come, like so many pilgrims of old, from
the banks of the Nile to visit the sanctuaries of
Osiris, which lie beyond the green plains, on the
edge of the desert.

It is a journey of some ten miles or so, under
a clear sky and a burning sun. We pass through
fields of corn and lucerne, whose wonderful
green is piqued with little flowers, such as may
be seen in our climate. Hundreds of little birds
sing to us distractedly of the joy of life; the sun
shines radiantly, magnificently; the impetuous
corn is already in the ear; it might be some gay
pageant of our days of May. One forgets that
it is February, that we are still in the winter—
the luminous winter of Egypt.

Here and there amongst the outspread fields
are villages buried under the thick foliage of
trees—under acacias which, in the distance, resemble ours at home; beyond indeed the mountain chain of Libya, like a wall confining the
fertile fields, looks strange perhaps in its rose-

colour, and too desolate; but, nevertheless, amidst
this glad music of the fields, these songs of larks
and twitterings of sparrows, you scarcely realise
that you are in a foreign land.

Abydos! what magic there is in the name!
"Abydos is at hand, and in another moment we
shall be there." The mere words seem somehow
to transform the aspect of the homely green
fields, and make this pastoral region almost imposing. The buzzing of the flies increases in
the overheated air and the song of the birds sub-
sides until at last it dies away in the approach
of noon.

We have been journeying a little more than
an hour amongst the verdure of the growing
corn that lies upon the fields like a carpet, when
suddenly, beyond the little houses and trees of
a village, quite a different world is disclosed—
the familiar world of glare and death which
presses so closely upon inhabited Egypt: the
desert! the desert of Libya, and now as ever
when we come upon it suddenly from the banks
of the old river, it rises up before us; beginning
at once, without transition, absolute and terrible, as soon as we leave the thick velvet of the
last field, the cool shade of the last acacia. Its
sands seem to slope towards us, in a prodigious
incline, from the strange mountains that we saw
from the happy plain, and which now appear,

enthroned beyond, like the monarchs of all this nothingness.

The town of Abydos, which has vanished and left no wrack behind, rose once in this spot where we now stand, on the very threshold of the solitudes; but its necropoles, more venerated even than those of Memphis, and its thrice-holy temples, are a little farther on, in the marvellously conserving sand, which has buried them under its tireless waves and preserved them almost intact up till the present day.

The desert! As soon as we put foot upon its shifting soil, which smothers the sound of our steps, the atmosphere too seems suddenly to change; it burns with a strange new heat, as if great fires had been lighted in the neighbourhood.

And this whole domain of light and drought, right away into the distance, is shaded and streaked with the familiar brown, red and yellow colours. The mournful reflection of adjacent things augments to excess the heat and light. The horizon trembles under the little vapours of mirage like water ruffled by the wind. The background, which mounts gradually to the foot of the Libyan mountains, is strewn with the debris of bricks and stones — shapeless ruins which, though they scarcely rise above the sand, abound nevertheless in great numbers, and serve to remind us that here indeed is a very ancient soil, where men laboured in centuries that have drifted out of knowledge. One divines instinctively and at once the catacombs, the hypogea and the mummies that lie beneath!

These necropoles of Abydos once—and for thousands of years—exercised an extraordinary fascination over this people—the precursor of peoples—who dwelt in the valley of the Nile. According to one of the most ancient of human traditions, the head of Osiris, the lord of the *other world*, reposed in the depths of one of the temples which to-day are buried in the sands. And men, as soon as their thought commenced to issue from the primeval night, were haunted by the idea that there were localities helpful, as it were, to the poor corpses that lay beneath the earth, that there were certain holy places where it behoved them to be buried if they wished to be ready when the signal of awakening was given. And in old Egypt, therefore, each one, at the hour of death, turned his thoughts to these stones and sands, in the ardent hope that he might be able to sleep near the remains of his god. And when the place was becoming crowded with sleepers, those who could obtain no place there conceived the idea of having humble obelisks planted on the holy ground, which at least should tell their names; or even recommended that their mummies might lie

there for some weeks, even if they were afterwards removed. And thus, funeral processions
passed to and fro without ceasing through the
cornfields that separate the Nile from the desert.
Abydos! In the sad human dream dominated
by the thought of dissolution, Abydos preceded
by many centuries the Valley of Jehosophat of
the Hebrews, the cemeteries around Mecca of the
Moslems, and the holy tombs beneath our oldest
cathedrals! . . . Abydos! It behoves us to walk
here pensively and silently out of respect for all
those thousands of souls who formerly turned
towards this place, with outstretched hands, in
the hour of death.

The first great temple—that which King Seti
raised to the mysterious Prince of the Other
World, who in those days was called Osiris—is
quite close—a distance of little more than 200
yards in the glare of the desert. We come
upon it suddenly, so that it almost startles us,
for nothing warns us of its proximity. The
sand from which it has been exhumed, and which
buried it for 2000 years, still rises almost to its
roof. Through an iron gate, guarded by two
tall Bedouin guards in black robes, we plunge
at once into the shadow of enormous stones.
We are in the house of the god, in a forest of
heavy Osiridean columns, surrounded by a world
of people in high coiffures, carved in bas-relief

on the pillars and walls—people who seem to be signalling one to another and exchanging amongst themselves mysterious signs, silently and for ever.

But what is this noise in the sanctuary? It seems to be full of people. There, sure enough, beyond a second row of columns, is quite a little crowd talking loudly in English. I fancy that I can hear the clinking of glasses and the tapping of knives and forks.

Oh! poor, poor temple, to what strange uses are you come. . . . This excess of grotesqueness in profanation is more insulting surely than to be sacked by barbarians! Behold a table set for some thirty guests, and the guests themselves—of both sexes—merry and lighthearted, belong to that special type of humanity which patronises Thomas Cook & Son (Egypt Ltd.). They wear cork helmets, and the classic green spectacles; drink whisky and soda, and eat voraciously sandwiches and other viands out of greasy paper, which now litters the floor. And the women! Heavens! what scarecrows they are! And this kind of thing, so the black-robed Bedouin guards inform us, is repeated every day so long as the season lasts. A luncheon in the temple of Osiris is part of the programme of pleasure trips. Each day at noon a new band arrives, on heedless and unfortunate donkeys.

The tables and the crockery remain, of course, in the old temple!

Let us escape quickly, if possible before the sight shall have become graven on our memory.

But alas! even when we are outside, alone again on the expanse of dazzling sands, we can no longer take things seriously.   Abydos and the desert have ceased to exist.   The faces of those women remain to haunt us, their faces and their hats, and those looks which they vouchsafed us from over their solar spectacles. . . . The ugliness associated with the name of Cook was once explained to me in this wise, and the explanation at first sight seemed satisfactory: " The United Kingdom, justifiably jealous of the beauty of its daughters, submits them to a jury when they reach the age of puberty; and those who are classed as too ugly to reproduce their kind are accorded an unlimited account at Thomas Cook & Sons, and thus vowed to a course of perpetual travel, which leaves them no time to think of certain trifles incidental to life."   The explanation, as I say, seduced me for the time being.   But a more attentive examination of the bands who infest the valley of the Nile enables me to aver that all these good English ladies are of an age notoriously canonical: and the catastrophe of procreation, therefore, supposing that such an accident could ever have happened to them, must date back to a time long anterior to their enrolment. And I remain perplexed!

Without conviction now, we make our way towards another temple, guaranteed solitary. Indeed the sun blazes there a lonely sovereign in the midst of a profound silence, and Egypt and the past take us again into their folds.

Once more to Osiris, the god of heavenly awakening in the necropolis of Abydos, this sanctuary was built by Ramses II. But the sands have covered it with their winding sheet in vain, and have been able to preserve for us only the lower and more deeply buried parts. Men in their blind greed have destroyed the upper portions,[1] and its ruins, protected and cleared as they are to-day, rise only some ten or twelve feet from the ground. In the bas-reliefs the majority of the figures have only legs and a portion of the body; their heads and shoulders have disappeared with the upper parts of the walls. But they seem to have preserved their vitality: the gesticulations, the exaggerated pantomime of the attitudes of these headless things, are more strange, more striking,

[1] Not long ago a manufacturer, established in the neigh-bourhood, discovering that the limestone of its walls was friable, used this temple as a quarry, and for some years bas-reliefs beyond price served as aliment to the mills of the factory.

perhaps, than if their faces still remained. And
they have preserved too, in an extraordinary
degree, the brightness of their antique paintings,
the fresh tints of their costumes, of their robes
of turquoise blue, or lapis, or emerald-green, or
golden-yellow. It is an artless kind of fresco-
work, which nevertheless amazes us by remain-
ing perfect after thirty-five centuries. All that
these people did seems as if made for immortality. It is true, however, that such brilliant colours are not found in any of the other Pharaonic
monuments, and that here they are heightened
by the white background. For, notwithstanding
the bluish, black and red granite of the porticoes,
the walls are all of a fine limestone, of exceeding
whiteness, and, in the holy of holies, of a pure
alabaster.

Above the truncated walls, with their bright
clear colours, the desert appears, and shows quite
brown by contrast; one sees the great yellow
swell of sand and stones above the pictures of
these decapitated people. It rises like a colossal
wave and stretches out to bathe the foot of the
Libyan mountains beyond. Towards the north
and west of the solitudes, shapeless ruins of
tawny-coloured blocks follow one another in the
sands until the dazzling distance ends in a clear-
cut line against the sky. Apart from this temple of Ramses, where we now stand, and that

of Seti in the vicinity, where the enterprise of
Thomas Cook & Son flourishes, there is nothing
around us but ruins, crumbled and pulverised
beyond all possible redemption. But they give
us pause, these disappearing ruins, for they are
the debris of that ageless temple, where sleeps
the head of the god, the debris of the tombs of
the Middle and Ancient Empires, and they indi-
cate still the wide extent and development of the
necropoles of Abydos, so old that it almost makes
one giddy to think of their beginning.

Here, as at Thebes and Memphis, the tombs
of the Egyptians are met with only amongst
the sands and the parched rocks. The great
ancestral people, who would have shuddered at
our black trees, and the corruption of the damp
graves, liked to place its embalmed dead in the
midst of this luminous, changeless splendour of
death, which men call the desert.

．　　　．　　　．　　　．　　　．　　　．　　　．

And what is this now that is happening in
the holy neighbourhood of unhappy Osiris? A
troupe of donkeys, belaboured by Bedouin
drivers, is being driven in the direction of the
adjacent temple, dedicated to the god by Seti!
The luncheon no doubt is over and the band
about to depart, sharp to the appointed hour
of the programme. Let us watch them from a
prudent distance.

To be brief, they all mount into their saddles, these Cooks and Cookesses, and opening, not without a conscious air of majesty, their white cotton parasols, take themselves off in the direction of the Nile. They disappear and the place belongs to us.

When we venture at last to return to the first sanctuary, where they had lunched their fill in the shade, the guardians are busy clearing away the leavings and the dirty paper. And they pack the dubious crockery, which will be required for to-morrow's luncheon, into large chests on which may be read in large letters of glory the names of the veritable sovereigns of modern Egypt: " Thomas Cook & Son (Egypt Ltd.)."

All this happily ends with the first hypostyle. Nothing dishonours the halls of the interior, where silence has again descended, the vast silence of the noon of the desert.

In the reign of the Emperor Tiberius, men already marvelled at this temple, as at a relic of the most distant and nebulous past. The geographer Strabo wrote in those days: " It is an admirable palace built in the fashion of the Labyrinth save that it has fewer galleries." There are galleries enough however, and one can readily lose oneself in its mazy turnings. Seven chapels, consecrated to Osiris and to different

gods and goddesses of his suite; seven vaulted
chambers; seven doors for the processions of
kings and multitudes; and, at the sides, numberless halls, corridors, secondary chapels, dark
chambers and hidden doorways. That very
primitive column, suggestive of reeds, which is
called in architecture the "plant column" and
resembles a monstrous stem of the papyrus, rises
here in a thick forest, to support the stones of
the blue ceilings, which are strewn with stars, in
the likeness of the sky of this country. In many
cases these stones are missing and leave large
openings on to the real sky above. Their
massiveness, which one might have thought
would secure them an endless duration, has
availed them nothing; the sun of so many
centuries has cracked them, and their own
weight, then, has brought them headlong to
the ground. And floods of light now enter
through the gaps, into the very chapels where
the men of old had thought to ensure a holy
gloom.

Despite the disaster which has overtaken the
ceilings, this is nevertheless one of the most
perfect of the sanctuaries of ancient Egypt.
The sands, those gentle sextons, have here succeeded miraculously in their work of preservation. They might have been carved yesterday,
these innumerable people, who, everywhere—on

the walls, on this forest of columns—gesticulate
and, with their arms and long hands, continue
with animation their eternal mute conversation.
The whole temple, with the openings which
give it light, is more beautiful perhaps than
in the time of the Pharaohs. In place of the
old-time darkness, a transparent gloom now
alternates with shafts of sunlight. Here and
there the subjects of the bas-reliefs, so long
buried in the darkness, are deluged with burning
rays which detail their attitudes, their muscles,
their scarcely altered colours, and endow them
again with life and youth. There is no part of
the wall, in this immense place, but is covered
with divinities, with hieroglyphs and emblems.
Osiris in high coiffure, the beautiful Isis in the
helmet of a bird, jackal-headed Anubis, falcon-
headed Horus, and ibis-headed Thoth are repeated a thousand times, welcoming with strange
gestures the kings and priests who are rendering
them homage.

The bodies, almost nude, with broad shoulders
and slim waist, have a slenderness, a grace,
infinitely chaste, and the features of the faces
are of an exquisite purity. The artists who
carved these charming heads, with their long
eyes, full of the ancient dream, were already
skilled in their art; but through a deficiency,
which puzzles us, they were only able to draw

them in profile. All the legs, all the feet are
in profile too, although the bodies, on the
other hand, face us fully. Men needed yet some
centuries of study before they understood perspective—which to us now seems so simple—
and the foreshortening of figures, and were able
to render the impression of them on a plane
surface.

Many of the pictures represent King Seti,
drawn without doubt from life, for they show
us almost the very features of his mummy, ex-
hibited now in the museum at Cairo. At his
side he holds affectionately his son, the prince-
royal, Ramses (later on Ramses II., the great
Sesostris of the Greeks). They have given the
latter quite a frank air, and he wears a curl on
the side of his head, as was the fashion then in
childhood. He, also, has his mummy in a glass
case in the museum, and anyone who has seen
that toothless, sinister wreck, who had already
attained the age of nearly a hundred years
before death delivered him to the embalmers of
Thebes, will find it difficult to believe that he
could ever have been young, and worn his hair
curled so; that he could even have played and
been a child.

.   .   .   .

We thought we had finished with the Cooks
and Cookesses of the luncheon. But alas! our

horses, faster than their donkeys, overtake them in the return journey amongst the green corn-fields of Abydos; and in a stoppage in the narrow roadway, caused by a meeting with a number of camels laden with lucerne, we are brought to a halt in their midst.   Almost touching me is a dear little white donkey, who looks at me pensively and in such a way that we at once understand one another.   A mutual sympathy unites us.   A Cookess in spectacles surmounts him—the most hideous of them all, bony and severe.   Over her travelling costume, already sufficiently repulsive, she wears a tennis jersey, which accentuates the angularity of her figure, and in her person she seems the very incarnation of the respectability of the British Isles.   It would be more equitable, too—so long are those legs of hers, which, to be sure, have scant interest for the tourist—if she carried the donkey.

The poor little white thing regards me with melancholy.   His ears twitch restlessly and his beautiful eyes, so fine, so observant of every-thing, say to me as plain as words:

" She is a beauty, isn't she? "

" She is, indeed, my poor little donkey.   But think of this: fixed on thy back as she is, thou hast this advantage over me—thou seest her not! "

But my reflection, though judicious enough, does not console him, and his look answers me that he would be much prouder if he carried, like so many of his comrades, a simple pack of sugar-canes.

THE DOWNFALL
OF THE NILE

CHAPTER XI

SOME thousands of years ago, at the beginning of our geological period, when the continents had taken, in the last great upheaval, almost the forms by which we now know them, and when the rivers began to trace their hesitating courses, it happened that the rains of a whole watershed of Africa were precipitated in one formidable torrent across the uninhabitable region which stretches from the Atlantic to the Indian Ocean, and is called the region of the deserts. And this enormous waterway, lost as it was in the sands, by-and-by regulated its course: it became the Nile, and with untiring patience set itself to its proper task of river, which in this accursed zone might well have seemed an impossible one. First it had to round all the blocks of granite scattered in its way in the high plains of Nubia; and then, and more especially, to deposit, little by little, successive layers of mud, to form a living artery, to create, as it were, a long, green ribbon in the midst of this infinite domain of death.

How long ago is it since the work of the great

149

river began? There is something fearful in the thought. During the 5000 years of which we have any knowledge the incessant deposit of mud has scarcely widened this strip of inhabited Egypt, which at the most ancient period of history was almost as it is to-day. And as for the granite blocks on the plains of Nubia, how many thousands of years did it need to roll them and to polish them thus? In the times of the Pharaohs they already had their present rounded forms, worn smooth by the friction of the water, and the hieroglyphic inscriptions on their surfaces are not perceptibly effaced, though they have suffered the periodical inundation of the summer for some forty or fifty centuries!

It was an exceptional country, this valley of the Nile; marvellous and unique; fertile without rain, watered according to its need by the great river, without the help of any cloud. It knew not the dull days and the humidity under which we suffer, but kept always the changeless sky of the immense surrounding deserts, which exhaled no vapour that might dim the horizon. It was this eternal splendour of its light, no doubt, and this easiness of life, which brought forth here the first fruits of human thought. This same Nile, after having so patiently created the soil of Egypt, became also the father of that people, which led the way for all the others—like those early branches that one sees in spring, which shoot first from the stem, and sometimes die before the summer. It nursed that people, whose least vestiges we discover to-day with surprise and wonder; a people who, in the very dawn, in the midst of the original barbarity, conceived magnificently the infinite and the divine; who placed with such certainty and grandeur the first architectural lines, from which afterwards our architecture was to be derived; who laid the bases of art, of science, and of all knowledge.

Later on, when this beautiful flower of humanity was faded, the Nile, flowing always in the midst of its deserts, seems to have had for mission, during nearly two thousand years, the maintenance on its banks of a kind of immobility and desuetude, which was in a way a homage of respect for these stupendous relics. While the sand was burying the ruins of the temples and the battered faces of the colossi, nothing changed under this sky of changeless blue. The same cultivation proceeded on the banks as in the oldest ages; the same boats, with the same sails, went up and down the thread of water; the same songs kept time to the eternal human toil. The race of fellahs, the unconscious guardian of a prodigious past, slept on without desire of change, and almost without suffering. And time passed for Egypt in a great peace of sunlight and of death.

But to-day the foreigners are masters here, and have wakened the old Nile—wakened to enslave it. In less than twenty years they have disfigured its valley, which until then had preserved itself like a sanctuary. They have silenced its cataracts, captured its precious water by dams, to pour it afar off on plains that are become like marshes and already sully with their mists the crystal clearness of the sky. The ancient rigging no longer suffices to water the land under cultivation. Machines worked by steam, which draw the water more quickly, commence to rise along the banks, side by side with new factories. Soon there will scarcely be a river more dishonoured than this, by iron chimneys and thick, black smoke. And it is happening apace, this exploitation of the Nile—hastily, greedily, as in a hunt for spoils. And thus all its beauty disappears, for its monotonous course, through regions endlessly alike, won us only by its calm and its old-world mystery.

Poor Nile of the prodigies! One feels sometimes still its departing charm, stray corners of it remain intact. There are days of transcendent clearness, incomparable evenings, when one may still forget the ugliness and the smoke. But the classic expedition by dahabiya, the ascent of the river from Cairo to Nubia, will soon have ceased to be worth making.

Ordinarily this voyage is made in the winter,
so that the traveller may follow the course of the
sun as it makes its escape towards the southern
hemisphere. The water then is low and the
valley parched. Leaving the cosmopolitan town
of modern Cairo, the iron bridges, and the pretentious hotels, with their flaunting inscriptions,
it imparts a sense of sudden peacefulness to pass
along the large and rapid waters of this river,
between the curtains of palm-trees on the banks,
borne by a dahabiya where one is master and, if
one likes, may be alone.

At first, for a day or two, the great haunting
triangles of the pyramids seem to follow you,
those of Dashur and that of Sakkarah succeeding
to those of Gizeh. For a long time the horizon
is disturbed by their gigantic silhouettes. As
we recede from them, and they disengage themselves better from neighbouring things, they
seem, as happens in the case of mountains, to
grow higher. And when they have finally disappeared, we have still to ascend slowly and by
stages some six hundred miles of river before we
reach the first cataract. Our way lies through
monotonous desert regions where the hours and
days are marked chiefly by the variations of the
wonderful light. Except for the phantasmagoria
of the mornings and evenings, there is no out-
standing feature on these dull-coloured banks,

where may be seen, with never a change at all, the humble pastoral life of the fellahs. The sun is burning, the starlit nights clear and cold. A withering wind, which blows almost without ceasing from the north, makes you shiver as soon as the twilight falls.

One may travel for league after league along this slimy water and make head for days and weeks against its current—which glides everlastingly past the dahabiya, in little hurrying waves—without seeing this warm, fecundating river, compared with which our rivers of France are mere negligible streams, either diminish or increase or hasten. And on the right and left of us as we pass are unfolded indefinitely the two parallel chains of barren limestone, which imprison so narrowly the Egypt of the harvests: on the west that of the Libyan desert, which every morning the first rays of the sun tint with a rosy coral that nothing seems to dull; and in the east that of the desert of Arabia, which never fails in the evening to retain the light of the setting sun, and looks then like a mournful girdle of glowing embers. Sometimes the two parallel walls sheer off and give more room to the green fields, to the woods of palm-trees, and the little oases, separated by streaks of golden sand. Sometimes they approach so closely to the Nile that habitable Egypt is no wider than some two or three poor fields of corn, lying right on the water's edge, behind which the dead stones and the dead sands commence at once. And sometimes, even, the desert chain closes in so as to overhang the river with its reddish-white cliffs, which no rain ever comes to freshen, and in which, at different heights, gape the square holes leading to the habitations of the mummies. These mountains, which in the distance look so beautiful in their rose-colour, and make, as it were, interminable back-cloths to all that happens on the river banks, were perforated, during some 5000 years, for the introduction of sarcophagi and now they swarm with old dead bodies.

And all that passes on the banks, indeed, changes as little as the background.

First there is that gesture, supple and superb, but always the same, of the women in their long black robes who come without ceasing to fill their long-necked jars and carry them away balanced on their veiled heads. Then the flocks which shepherds, draped in mourning, bring to the river to drink, goats and sheep and asses all mixed up together. And then the buffaloes, massive and mud-coloured, who descend calmly to bathe. And, finally, the great labour of the watering: the traditional noria, turned by a little bull with bandaged eyes and, above all, the shadûf, worked by men whose naked bodies stream with the cold water.

The shadûfs follow one another sometimes as far as the eye can see. It is strange to watch the movement—confused in the distance—of all these long rods which pump the water without ceasing, and look like the swaying of living antennæ. The same sight was to be seen along this river in the times of the Ramses. But suddenly, at some bend of the river, the old Pharaonic rigging disappears, to give place to a succession of steam machines, which, more even than the muscles of the fellahs, are busy at the water-drawing. Before long their blackish chimneys will make a continuous border to the tamed Nile.

Did one not know their bearings, the great ruins of this Egypt would pass unnoticed. With a few rare exceptions they lie beyond the green plains on the threshold of the solitudes. And against the changeless, rose-coloured background of these cliffs of the desert, which follow you during the whole of this tranquil navigation of some 600 miles, are to be seen only the humble towns and villages of to-day, which have the neutral colour of the ground. Some openwork minarets dominate them—white spots above the prevailing dulness. Clouds of pigeons whirl round in the neighbourhood. And amongst the

little houses, which are only cubes of mud, baked
in the sun, the palm-trees of Africa, either singly
or in mighty clusters, rise superbly and cast on
these little habitations the shade of their palms
which sway in the wind. Not long ago, although
indeed everything in these little towns was
mournful and stagnant, one would have been
tempted to stop in passing, drawn by that nameless peace that belonged to the Old East and to
Islam. But, now, before the smallest hamlet—
amongst the beautiful primitive boats, that still
remain in great numbers, pointing their yards,
like very long reeds, into the sky—there is always,
for the meeting of the tourist boats, an enormous
black pontoon, which spoils the whole scene by
its presence and its great advertising inscription:
" Thomas Cook & Son (Egypt Ltd.)." And,
what is more, one hears the whistling of the railway, which runs mercilessly along the river,
bringing from the Delta to the Soudan the hordes
of European invaders. And to crown all, adjoining the station is inevitably some modern
factory, throned there in a sort of irony, and
dominating the poor crumbling things that still
presume to tell of Egypt and of mystery.

And so now, except at the towns or villages
which lead to celebrated ruins, we stop no longer.
It is necessary to proceed farther and for the
halt of the night to seek an obscure hamlet, a

silent recess, where we may moor our dahabiya
against the venerable earth of the bank.

And so one goes on, for days and weeks,
between these two interminable cliffs of reddish
chalk, filled with their hypogea and mummies,
which are the walls of the valley of the Nile,
and will follow us up to the first cataract, until
our entrance into Nubia. There only will the
appearance and nature of the rocks of the desert
change, to become the more sombre granite
out of which the Pharaohs carved their obelisks
and the great figures of their gods.

We go on and on, ascending the thread of this
eternal current, and the regularity of the wind,
the persistent clearness of the sky, the monotony
of the great river, which winds but never ends,
all conspire to make us forget the hours and days
that pass. However deceived and disappointed
we may be at seeing the profanation of the river
banks, here, nevertheless, isolated on the water,
we do not lose the peace of being a wanderer, a
stranger amongst an equipage of silent Arabs,
who every evening prostrate themselves in con-
fiding prayer.

And, moreover, we are moving towards the
south, towards the sun, and every day has a more
entrancing clearness, a more caressing warmth,
and the bronze of the faces that we see on our
way takes on a deeper tint.

And then too one mixes intimately with the
life of the river bank, which is still so absorbing
and, at certain hours, when the horizon is un-
sullied by the smoke of pit-coal, recalls you to
the days of artless toil and healthy beauty. In
the boats that meet us, half-naked men, revelling
in their movement, in the sun and air, sing, as
they ply their oars, those songs of the Nile that
are as old as Thebes or Memphis. When the
wind rises there is a riotous unfurling of sails,
which, stretched on their long yards, give to
the dahabiyas the air of birds in full flight.
Bending right over in the wind, they skim along
with a lively motion, carrying their cargoes of
men and beasts and primitive things. Women
are there draped still in the ancient fashion, and
sheep and goats, and sometimes piles of fruit
and gourds, and sacks of grain. Many are laden
to the water's edge with those earthenware jars,
unchanged for 3000 years, which the fellaheens
know how to place on their heads with so much
grace—and one sees these heaps of fragile pottery
gliding along the water as if carried by the
gigantic wings of a gull. And in the far-off, almost fabulous, days the life of the mariners of the
Nile had the same aspect, as is shown by the bas-
reliefs on the oldest tombs; it required the same
play of muscles and of sails; was accompanied
no doubt by the same songs, and was subject to

the withering caress of this same desert wind.
And then, as now, the same unchanging rose coloured the continuous curtain of the mountains.

But all at once there is a noise of machinery,
and whistlings, and in the air, which was just
now so pure, rise noxious columns of black
smoke. The modern steamers are coming, and
throw into disorder the flotillas of the past:
colliers that leave great eddies in their wake, or
perhaps a wearisome lot of those three-decked
tourist boats, which make a great noise as they
plough the water, and are laden for the most
part with ugly women, snobs and imbeciles.

Poor, poor Nile! which reflected formerly on
its warm mirror the utmost of earthly splendour,
which bore in its time so many barques of gods
and goddesses in procession behind the golden
barge of Amen, and knew in the dawn of the
ages only an impeccable purity, alike of the
human form and of architectural design! What
a downfall is here! To be awakened from
that disdainful sleep of twenty centuries and
made to carry the floating barracks of Thomas
Cook & Son, to feed sugar factories, and to ex-
haust itself in nourishing with its mud the raw
material for English cotton-stuffs.

IN THE TEMPLE OF THE
GODDESS OF LOVE AND JOY

CHAPTER XII

IN THE TEMPLE OF THE GODDESS OF LOVE
AND JOY

IT is the month of March, but as gay and splendid as in our June. Around us are fields of corn, of lucerne, and the flowering bean. And the air is full of restless birds, singing deliriously for very joy in the voluptuous business of their nests and coveys. Our way lies over a fertile soil, saturated with vital substances— some paradise for beasts no doubt, for they swarm on every side: flocks of goats with a thousand bleating kids; she-asses with their frisking young; cows and cow-buffaloes feeding their calves; all turned loose among the crops, to browse at their leisure, as if there were here a superabundance of the riches of the soil.

What country is this that shows no sign of human habitation, that knows no village, nor any distant spire? The crops are like ours at home—wheat, lucerne, and the flowering bean that perfumes the air with its white blossoms. But there is an excess of light in the sky and, in the distance, an extraordinary clearness. And then these fertile plains, that might be

163

those of some "Promised Land," seem to be bounded far away, on left and right, by two parallel stone walls, two chains of rose-coloured mountains, whose aspect is obviously desertlike. Besides, amongst the numerous animals that are familiar, there are camels, feeding their strange nurslings that look like four-legged ostriches. And finally some peasants appear beyond in the cornfields; they are veiled in long black draperies. It is the East then, an African land, or some oasis of Arabia?

The sun at this moment is hidden from us by a band of clouds, that stretches, right above our head, from one end of the sky to the other, like a long skein of white wool. It is alone in the blue void, and seems to make more peaceful, and even a little mysterious, the wonderful light of the fields we traverse—these fields intoxicated with life and vibrant with the music of birds; while, by contrast, the distant landscape, un-shaded by clouds, is resplendent with a more incisive clearness and the desert beyond seems deluged with rays.

The pathway that we have been following, ill defined as it is in the grassy fields, leads us at length under a large ruinous portico—a relic of goodness knows what olden days—which still rises here, quite isolated, altogether strange and unexpected, in the midst of the green expanse

of pasture and tillage. We had seen it from
a great distance, so pure and clear is the air;
and in approaching it we perceive that it is
colossal, and in relief on its lintel is designed
a globe with two long wings outspread symmetrically.

It behoves us now to make obeisance with
almost religious reverence, for this winged disc
is a symbol which gives at length an indication
of the place immediate and absolute.   It is
Egypt, the country—Egypt, our ancient mother.
And there before us must once have stood a
temple reverenced of the people, or some great
vanished town; its fragments of columns and
sculptured capitals are strewn about in the fields
of lucerne.   How inexplicable it seems that
this land of ancient splendours, which never
ceased indeed to be nutritive and prodigiously
fertile, should have returned, for some hundreds
of years now, to the humble pastoral life of the
peasants.

Through the green crops and the assembled
herds our pathway seems to lead to a kind of hill
rising alone in the midst of the plains—a hill
which is neither of the same colour nor the same
nature as the mountains of the surrounding deserts.   Behind us the portico recedes little by little in the distance; its tall imposing silhouette,
so mournful and solitary, throws an infinite sad-

ness on this sea of meadows, which spread
their peace where once was a centre of magnificence.

The wind now rises in sharp, lashing gusts
—the wind of Egypt that never seems to fall,
and is bitter and wintry for all the burning of
the sun. The growing corn bends before it,
showing the gloss of its young quivering leaves,
and the herded beasts move close to one another
and turn their backs to the squall.

As we draw nearer to this singular hill it is
revealed as a mass of ruins. And the ruins are
all of a kind, of a brownish-red. They are the remains of the colonial towns of the Romans, which
subsisted here for some two or three hundred
years (an almost negligible moment of time in
the long history of Egypt), and then fell to
pieces, to become in time mere shapeless mounds
on the fertile margins of the Nile and sometimes
even in the submerging sands.

A heap of little reddish bricks that once were
fashioned into houses; a heap of broken jars
or amphoræ—myriads of them—that served to
carry the water from the old nourishing river;
and the remains of walls, repaired at diverse
epochs, where stones inscribed with hieroglyphs
lie upside down against fragments of Grecian
obelisks or Coptic sculptures or Roman capitals.
In our countries, where the past is of yesterday,

we have nothing resembling such a chaos of dead things.

Nowadays the sanctuary is reached through a large cutting in this hill of ruins; incredible heaps of bricks and broken pottery enclose it on all sides like a jealous rampart. Until recently indeed they covered it almost to its roof. From the very first its appearance is disconcerting: it is so grand, so austere and gloomy. A strange dwelling, to be sure, for the Goddess of Love and Joy. It seems more fit to be the home of the Prince of Darkness and of Death. A severe doorway, built of gigantic stones and surmounted by a winged disc, opens on to an asylum of religious mystery, on to depths where massive columns disappear in the darkness of deep night.

Immediately on entering there is a coolness and a resonance as of a sepulchre. First, the pronaos, where we still see clearly, between pillars carved with hieroglyphs. Were it not for the large human faces which serve for the capitals of the columns, and are the image of the lovely Hathor, the goddess of the place, this temple of the decadent epoch would scarcely differ from those built in this country two thousand years before. It has the same square massiveness.

And in the dark blue ceilings there are the

same frescoes, filled with stars, with the signs of
the Zodiac, and series of winged discs; in bas-
relief on the walls, the same multitudinous crowds
of people who gesticulate and make signs to
one another with their hands—eternally the same
mysterious signs, repeated to infinity, everywhere
—in the palaces, the hypogea, the syringes, and
on the sarcophagi and papyri of the mummies.

The Memphite and Theban temples, which
preceded this by so many centuries, and far
surpassed it in grandeur, have all lost, in consequence of the falling of the enormous granites
of their roofs, their cherished gloom, and, what is
the same thing, their religious mystery. But in
the temple of the lovely Hathor, on the contrary, except for some figures mutilated by the
hammers of Christians or Moslems, everything
has remained intact, and the lofty ceilings still
throw their fearsome shadows.

The gloom deepens in the hypostyle which
follows the pronaos. Then come, one after
another, two halls of increasing holiness, where
the daylight enters regretfully through narrow
loopholes, barely lighting the superposed rows of
innumerable figures that gesticulate on the walls.
And then, after other majestic corridors, we reach
the heart of this heap of terrible stones, the holy
of holies, enveloped in deep gloom. The hieroglyphic inscriptions name this place the " Hall

of Mystery " and formerly the high priest *alone, and he only once in each year,* had the right to enter it for the performance of some now un-known rites.

The " Hall of Mystery " is empty to-day, despoiled long since of the emblems of gold and precious stones that once filled it.   The meagre little flames of the candles we have lit scarcely pierce the darkness which thickens over our heads towards the granite ceilings; at the most they only allow us to distinguish on the walls of the vast rectangular cavern the serried ranks of figures who exchange among themselves their dis-concerting mute conversations.

Towards the end of the ancient and at the beginning of the Christian era, Egypt, as we know, still exercised such a fascination over the world, by its ancestral prestige, by the memory of its dominating past, and the sovereign per-manence of its ruins, that it imposed its gods upon its conquerors, its handwriting, its archi-tecture, nay, even its religious rites and its mummies.   The Ptolemies built temples here, which reproduce those of Thebes and Abydos. Even the Romans, although they had already discovered the *vault,* followed here the primitive models, and continued those granite ceilings, made of monstrous slabs, placed flat, like our beams.   And so this temple of Hathor, built though it was in the time of Cleopatra and Augustus, on a site venerable in the oldest antiquity, recalls at first sight some conception of the Ramses.

If, however, you examine it more closely, there appears, particularly in the thousands of figures in bas-relief, a considerable divergence. The poses are the same indeed, and so too are the traditional gestures. But the exquisite grace of line is gone, as well as the hieratic calm of the expressions and the smiles. In the Egyptian art of the best periods the slender figures are as pure as the flowers they hold in their hands; their muscles may be indicated in a precise and skilful manner, but they remain, for all that, immaterial. The god Amen himself, the pro-creator, drawn often with an absolute crudity, would seem chaste compared with the hosts of this temple. For here, on the contrary, the figures might be those of living people, palpitating and voluptuous, who had posed themselves for sport in these consecrated attitudes. The throat of the beautiful goddess, her hips, her un-veiled nakedness, are portrayed with a searching and lingering realism; the flesh seems almost to quiver. She and her spouse, the beautiful Horus, son of Isis, contemplate each other there, naked, one before the other, and their laughing eyes are intoxicated with love.

Around the holy of holies is a number of halls, in deep shadow and massive as so many fortresses. They were used formerly for mysterious and complicated rites, and in them, as everywhere else, there is no corner of the wall but is overloaded with figures and hieroglyphs. Bats are asleep in the blue ceilings, where the winged discs, painted in fresco, look like flights of birds; and the hornets of the neighbouring fields have built their nests there in hundreds, so that they hang like stalactites.

Several staircases lead to the vast terraces formed by the great roofs of the temple—staircases narrow, stifling and dimly lighted by loopholes that reveal the heart-breaking thickness of the walls. And here again are the inevitable rows of figures, carved on all the walls, in the same familiar attitudes; they mount with us as we ascend, making all the time the self-same signs one to another.

As we emerge on to the roofs, bathed now in Egyptian sunlight and swept by a cold and bitter wind, we are greeted by a noise as of an aviary. It is the kingdom of the sparrows, who have built their nests in thousands in this temple of the complaisant goddess. They twitter now all together and with all their might out of very joy of living. It is an esplanade, this roof—a solitude paved with gigantic flagstones. From it we see,

beyond the heaps of ruins, those happy plains,
which are spread out with such a perfectly serenity on the very ground where once stood the
town of Denderah, beloved of Hathor and one
of the most famous of Upper Egypt. Exquisitely
green are these plains with the new growth of
wheat and lucerne and bean; and the herds
that are grouped here and there on the fresh
verdure of the level pastures, swaying now and
undulating in the wind, look like so many dark
patches. And the two chains of mountains of
rose-coloured stone, that run parallel—on the
east that of the desert of Arabia, on the west
that of the Libyan desert—enclose, in the distance, this valley of the Nile, this land of plenty,
which, alike in antiquity as in our days, has ex-
cited the greed of predatory races. The temple
has also some underground dependencies or
crypts into which you descend by staircases as of
dungeons; sometimes even you have to crawl
through holes to reach them. Long superposed
galleries which might serve as hiding places for
treasure; long corridors recalling those which, in
bad dreams, threaten to close in and bury you.
And the innumerable figures, of course, are here
too, gesticulating on the walls; and endless representations of the lovely goddess, whose swelling bosom, which has preserved almost intact the flesh colour applied in the times of

the Ptolemies, we have perforce to graze as we
pass.

.　　.　　.　　.　　.　　.　　.

In one of the vestibules that we have to traverse on our way out of the sanctuary, amongst
the numerous bas-reliefs representing various
sovereigns paying homage to the beautiful
Hathor, is one of a young man, crowned with a
royal tiara shaped like the head of a uræus. He
is shown seated in the traditional Pharaonic pose
and is none other than the Emperor Nero!

The hieroglyphs of the cartouche are there
to affirm his identity, albeit the sculptor, not
knowing his actual physiognomy, has given him
the traditional features, regular as those of the
god Horus. During the centuries of the Roman
domination the Western emperors used to send
from home instructions that their likeness should
be placed on the walls of the temples, and
that offerings should be made in their name to
the Egyptian divinities—and this notwithstanding that in their eyes Egypt must have seemed
so far away, a colony almost at the end of the
earth. (And it was such a goddess as this, of
secondary rank in the times of the Pharaohs, that
was singled out as the favourite of the Romans
of the decadence.)

The Emperor Nero! As a matter of fact at
the very time these bas-reliefs—almost the last

—and these expiring hieroglyphics were being inscribed, the confused primitive theogonies had almost reached their end and the days of the Goddess of Joy were numbered. There had been conceived in Judæa symbols more lofty and more pure, which were to rule a great part of the world for two thousand years—afterwards, alas, to decline in their turn; and men were about to throw themselves passionately into renunciation, asceticism and fraternal pity.

How strange it is to say it! Even while the sculptor was carving this archaic bas-relief, and was using, for the engraving of its name, characters that dated back to the night of the ages, there were already Christians assembled in the catacombs at Rome and dying in ecstasy in the arena!

MODERN LUXOR

CHAPTER XIII

THE waters of the Nile being already low, my dahabiya—delayed by strandings—had not been able to reach Luxor, and we had moored ourselves, as the darkness began to fall, at a casual spot on the bank.

"We are quite near," the pilot had told me before departing to make his evening prayer; "in an hour, to-morrow, we shall be there."

And the gentle night descended upon us in this spot which did not seem to differ at all from so many others where, for a month past now, we had moored our boat at hazard to await the daybreak. On the banks were dark confused masses of foliage, above which here and there a high date-palm outlined its black plumes. The air was filled with the multitudinous chirpings of the crickets of Upper Egypt, which make their music here almost throughout the year in the odorous warmth of the grass. And, presently, in the midst of the silence, rose the cries of the night birds, like the mournful mewings of cats. And that was all—save for the infinite calm of

the desert that is always present, dominating
everything, although scarcely noticed and, as it
were, latent.

.   .   .   .

And this morning, at the rising of the sun, is
pure and splendid as all other mornings. A tint
of rosy coral comes gradually to life on the
summit of the Libyan mountains, standing out
from the gridelin shadows which, in the heavens,
were the rearguard of the night.

But my eyes, grown accustomed during the
last few weeks to this glorious spectacle of the
dawn, turn themselves as if by force of some
attraction, towards a strange and quite unusual
thing, which, less than a mile away along the
river, on the Arabian bank, rises upright in the
midst of the mournful plains. At first it looks
like a mass of towering rocks, which in this hour
of twilight magic have taken on a pale violet
colour, and seem almost transparent. And the
sun, scarcely emerged from the desert, lights
them in a curious gradation, and borders their
contours with a fringe of fresh rose-colour. And
they are not rocks, in fact, for as we look more
closely, they show us lines symmetrical and
straight. Not rocks, but architectural masses,
tremendous and superhuman, placed there in
attitudes of quasi-eternal stability. And out of
them rise the points of two obelisks, sharp as the

blade of a lance. And then, at once, I understand—Thebes!

Thebes! Last evening it was hidden in the
shadow and I did not know it was so near. But
Thebes assuredly it is, for nothing else in the
world could produce such an apparition. And
I salute with a kind of shudder of respect this
unique and sovereign ruin, which had haunted
me for many years, but which until now life had
not left me time to visit.

And now for Luxor, which in the epoch of
the Pharaohs was a suburb of the royal town,
and is still its port. It is there, it seems, where
we must stop our dahabiya in order to proceed
to the fabulous palace which the rising sun has
just disclosed to us.

And while my equipage of bronze—intoning
that song, as old as Egypt and everlastingly the
same, which seems to help the men in their
arduous work—is busy unfastening the chain
which binds us to the bank, I continue to watch
the distant apparition. It emerges gradually
from the light morning mists which, perhaps,
made it seem even larger than it is. The clear
light of the ascending sun shows it now in
detail; and reveals it as all battered, broken and
ruinous in the midst of a silent plain, on the
yellow carpet of the desert. And how this sun,
rising in its clear splendour, seems to crush it

with its youth and stupendous duration. This
same sun had attained to its present round form,
had acquired the clear precision of its disc, and
begun its daily promenade over the country of
the sands, countless centuries of centuries, before it saw, as it might be yesterday, this town
of Thebes arise; an attempt at magnificence
which seemed to promise for the human pygmies
a sufficiently interesting future, but which, in
the event, we have not been able even to equal.
And it proved, too, a thing quite puny and
derisory, since here it is laid low, after having
subsisted barely four negligible thousands of
years.

.   .   .   .

An hour later we arrive at Luxor, and what
a surprise awaits us there!

The thing which dominates the whole town,
and may be seen five or six miles away, is the
Winter Palace, a hasty modern production which
has grown on the border of the Nile during the
past year: a colossal hotel, obviously sham, made
of plaster and mud, on a framework of iron.
Twice or three times as high as the admirable
Pharaonic temple, its impudent façade rises there,
painted a dirty yellow. One such thing, it will
readily be understood, is sufficient to disfigure
pitiably the whole of the surroundings. The old
Arab town, with its little white houses, its mina-

rets and its palm-trees, might as well not exist.
The famous temple and the forest of heavy
Osiridean columns admire themselves in vain
in the waters of the river. It is the end of
Luxor.

And what a crowd of people is here! While,
on the contrary, the opposite bank seems so
absolutely desertlike, with its stretches of golden
sand and, on the horizon, its mountains of the
colour of glowing embers, which, as we know, are
full of mummies.

Poor Luxor! Along the banks is a row of
tourist boats, a sort of two or three storeyed
barracks, which nowadays infest the Nile from
Cairo to the Cataracts. Their whistlings and the
vibration of their dynamos make an intolerable
noise. How shall I find a quiet place for my
dahabiya, where the functionaries of Messrs Cook
will not come to disturb me?

We can now see nothing of the palaces of
Thebes, whither I am to repair in the evening.
We are farther from them than we were last
night. The apparition during our morning's
journey had slowly receded in the plains flooded
by sunlight. And then the Winter Palace and
the new boats shut out the view.

But this modern quay of Luxor, where I dis-
embark at ten o'clock in the morning in clear and
radiant sunshine, is not without its amusing side.

In a line with the Winter Palace a number of stalls follow one another. All those things with which our tourists are wont to array themselves are on sale there: fans, fly flaps, helmets and blue spectacles. And, in thousands, photographs of the ruins. And there too are the toys, the souvenirs of the Soudan: old negro knives, panther-skins and gazelle horns. Numbers of Indians even are come to this improvised fair, bringing their stuffs from Rajputana and Cashmere. And, above all, there are dealers in mummies, offering for sale mysteriously shaped coffins, mummy-cloths, dead hands, gods, scarabæi —and the thousand and one things that this old soil has yielded for centuries like an inexhaustible mine.

Along the stalls, keeping in the shade of the houses and the scattered palms, pass representatives of the plutocracy of the world. Dressed by the same costumiers, bedecked in the same plumes, and with faces reddened by the same sun, the millionaire daughters of Chicago merchants elbow their sisters of the old nobility. Pressing amongst them impudent young Bedouins pester the fair travellers to mount their saddled donkeys. And as if they were charged to add to this babel a note of beauty, the battalions of Mr Cook, of both sexes, and always in a hurry, pass by with long strides.

Beyond the shops, following the line of the quay, there are other hotels. Less aggressive, all of them, than the Winter Palace, they have had the discretion not to raise themselves too high, and to cover their fronts with white chalk in the Arab fashion, even to conceal themselves in clusters of palm-trees.

And finally there is the colossal temple of Luxor, looking as out of place now as the poor obelisk which Egypt gave us as a present, and which stands to-day in the Place de la Concorde.

Bordering the Nile, it is a colossal grove of stone, about three hundred yards in length. In epochs of a magnificence that is now scarcely conceivable this forest of columns grew high and thick, rising impetuously at the bidding of Amenophis and the great Ramses. And how beautiful it must have been even yesterday, dominating in its superb disarray this surrounding country, vowed for centuries to neglect and silence!

But to-day, with all these things that men have built around it, you might say that it no longer exists.

We reach an iron-barred gate and, to enter, have to show our permit to the guards. Once inside the immense sanctuary, perhaps we shall find solitude again. But, alas, under the profaned columns a crowd of people passes, with *Baedekers* in their hands, the same people that one sees here everywhere, the same world as frequents Nice and the Riviera. And, to crown the mockery, the noise of the dynamos pursues us even here, for the boats of Messrs Cook are moored to the bank close by.

Hundreds of columns, columns which are anterior by many centuries to those of Greece, and represent, in their naive enormity, the first conceptions of the human brain. Some are fluted and give the impression of sheaves of monstrous reeds; others, quite plain and simple, imitate the stem of the papyrus, and bear by way of capital its strange flower. The tourists, like the flies, enter at certain times of the day, which it suffices to know. Soon the little bells of the hotels will call them away and the hour of midday will find me here alone. But what in heaven's name will deliver me from the noise of the dynamos? But look! beyond there, at the bottom of the sanctuaries, in the part which should be the holy of holies, that great fresco, now half effaced, but still clearly visible on the wall—how unexpected and arresting it is! An image of Christ! Christ crowned with the Byzantine aureole. It has been painted on a coarse plaster, which seems to have been added by an unskilful hand, and is wearing off and exposing the hieroglyphs beneath. . . .

This temple, in fact, almost indestructible by reason of its massiveness, has passed through the hands of diverse masters. Its antiquity was already legendary in the time of Alexander the Great, on whose behalf a chapel was added to it; and later on, in the first ages of Christianity, a corner of the ruins was turned into a cathedral. The tourists begin to depart, for the lunch bell calls them to the neighbouring *tables d'hôte*; and while I wait till they shall be gone, I occupy myself in following the bas-reliefs which are displayed for a length of more than a hundred yards along the base of the walls. It is one long row of people moving in their thousands all in the same direction—the ritual procession of the God Amen. With the care which characterised the Egyptians to draw everything from life so as to render it eternal, there are represented here the smallest details of a day of festival three or four thousand years ago. And how like it is to a holiday of the people of to-day! Along the route of the procession are ranged jugglers and sellers of drinks and fruits, and negro acrobats who walk on their hands and twist themselves into all kinds of contortions. But the procession itself was evidently of a magnificence such as we no longer know. The number of musicians and priests, of corporations, of emblems and banners, is quite bewildering. The God Amen himself came by

water, on the river, in his golden barge with
its raised prow, followed by the barques of all
the other gods and goddesses of his heaven. The
reddish stone, carved with minute care, tells me
all this, as it has already told it to so many dead
generations, so that I seem almost to see it.

And now everybody has gone: the colonnades
are empty and the noise of the dynamos has
ceased. Midday approaches with its torpor. The
whole temple seems to be ablaze with rays, and
I watch the clear-cut shadows cast by this forest
of stone gradually shortening on the ground.
The sun, which just now shone, all smiles and
gaiety, upon the quay of the new town amid the
uproar of the stall-keepers, the donkey drivers
and the cosmopolitan passengers, casts here a
sullen, impassive and consuming fire. And meanwhile the shadows shorten—and just as they do
every day, beneath this sky which is never overcast, just as they have done for five and thirty
centuries, these columns, these friezes, and this
temple itself, like a mysterious and solemn
sundial, record patiently on the ground the
slow passing of the hours. Verily for us, the
ephemeræ of thought, this unbroken continuity
of the sun of Egypt has more of melancholy
even than the changing, overcast skies of our
climate.

And now, at last, the temple is restored to

solitude and all noise in the neighbourhood has ceased.

An avenue bordered by very high columns, of which the capitals are in the form of the full-blown flowers of the papyrus, leads me to a place shut in and almost terrible, where is massed an assembly of colossi. Two, who, if they were standing, would be quite ten yards in height, are seated on thrones on either side of the entrance. The others, ranged on the three sides of the courtyard, stand upright behind colonnades, but look as if they were about to issue thence and to stride rapidly towards me. Some, broken and battered, have lost their faces and preserve only their intimidating attitude. Those that remain intact—white faces beneath their Sphinx's head-gear—open their eyes wide and smile.

This was formerly the principal entrance, and the office of these colossi was to welcome the multitudes. But now the gates of honour, flanked by obelisks of red granite, are obstructed by a litter of enormous ruins. And the courtyard has become a place voluntarily closed, where nothing of the outside world is any longer to be seen. In moments of silence, one can abstract oneself from all the neighbouring modern things, and forget the hour, the day, the century even, in the midst of these gigantic figures, whose smile disdains the flight of ages. The granites

within which we are immured—and in such
terrible company—shut out everything save the
point of an old neighbouring minaret which shows
now against the blue of the sky: a humble graft
of Islam which grew here amongst the ruins
some centuries ago, when the ruins themselves
had already subsisted for three thousand years—
a little mosque built on a mass of debris, which
it now protects with its inviolability. How many
treasures and relics and documents are hidden
and guarded by this mosque of the peristyle!
For none would dare to dig in the ground within
its sacred walls.

Gradually the silence of the temple becomes
profound. And if the shortened shadows betray
the hour of noon, there is nothing to tell to what
millennium that hour belongs. The silences and
middays like to this, which have passed before
the eyes of these giants ambushed in their colonnades—who could count them?

High above us, lost in the incandescent blue,
soar the birds of prey—and they were there in the
times of the Pharaohs, displaying in the air identical plumages, uttering the same cries. The
beasts and plants, in the course of time, have
varied less than men, and remain unchanged in
the smallest details.

Each of the colossi around me—standing there
proudly with one leg advanced as if for a march,

heavy and sure, which nothing should withstand —grasps passionately in his clenched fist, at the end of the muscular arm, a kind of buckled cross, which in Egypt was the symbol of eternal life. And this is what the decision of their movement symbolises: confident all of them in this poor bauble which they hold in their hand, they cross with a triumphant step the threshold of death. . . . " Eternal Life "—the thought of immortality—how the human soul has been obsessed by it, particularly in the periods marked by its greatest strivings! The tame submission to the belief that the rottenness of the grave is the end of all is characteristic of ages of decadence and mediocrity.

The three similar giants, little damaged in the course of their long existence, who align the eastern side of this courtyard strewn with blocks, represent, as indeed do all the others, that same Ramses II., whose effigy was multiplied so extravagantly at Thebes and Memphis. But these three have preserved a powerful and impetuous life. They might have been carved and polished yesterday. Between the monstrous reddish pillars, they look like white apparitions issuing from their embrasure of columns and advancing together like soldiers at manœuvres. The sun at this moment falls perpendicularly on their heads and strange headgear, details their everlasting smile, and then sheds itself on their

shoulders and their naked torso, exaggerating
their athletic muscles. Each holding in his hand
the symbolical cross, the three giants rush for-
ward with a formidable stride, heads raised, smil-
ing, in a radiant march into eternity.

Oh! this midday sun, that now pours down
upon the white faces of these giants, and dis-
places ever so slowly the shadows cast upon their
breasts by their chins and Osiridean beards. To
think how often in the midst of this same silence,
this same ray has fallen thus, fallen from the
same changeless sky, to occupy itself in this same
tranquil play! Yes, I think that the fogs and
rains of our winters, upon these stupendous ruins,
would be less sad and less terrible than the calm
of this eternal sunshine.

.   .   .   .

Suddenly a ridiculous noise begins to make
the air tremble; the dynamos of the Agencies
have been put in motion, and ladies in green
spectacles arrive, a charming throng, with guide-
books and cameras. The tourists, in short, are
come out of their hotels, at the same hour as the
flies awake. And the midday peace of Luxor
has come to an end.

A TWENTIETH - CENTURY
EVENING AT THEBES

CHAPTER XIV

An impalpable dust floats in a sky which scarcely ever knows a cloud; a dust so impalpable that, even while it powders the heavens with gold, it leaves them their infinite transparency. It is a dust of remote ages, of things destroyed; a dust that is here continually—of which the gold at this moment fades to green at the zenith, but flames and glistens in the west, for it is now that magnificent hour which marks the end of the day's decline, and the still burning globe of the sun, quite low down in the heaven, begins to light up on all sides the conflagration of the evening.

This setting sun illumines with splendour a silent chaos of granite, which is not that of the slipping of mountains, but that of ruins. And of such ruins as, to our eyes unaccustomed hereditarily to proportions so gigantic, seem superhuman. In places, huge masses of carven stone —pylons—still stand upright, rising like hills. Others are crumbling in all directions in bewildering cataracts of stone. It is difficult to conceive how these things, so massive that they might have

193

seemed eternal, could come to suffer such an utter
ruin.   Fragments of columns, fragments of
obelisks, broken by downfalls of which the mere
imagination is awful, heads and head-dresses of
giant divinities, all lie higgledy-piggledy in a
disorder beyond possible redress.   Nowhere surely
on our earth does the sun in his daily revolution
cast his light on such debris as this, on such a
litter of vanished palaces and dead colossi.

It was even here, seven or eight thousand
years ago, under this pure crystal sky, that the
first awakening of human thought began.   Our
Europe then was still sleeping, wrapped in the
mantle of its damp forests; sleeping that sleep
which still had thousands of years to run.   Here,
a precocious humanity, only recently emerged
from the Age of Stone, that earliest form of all,
an infant humanity, which saw massively on its
issue from the massiveness of the original matter,
conceived and built terrible sanctuaries for gods,
at first dreadful and vague, such as its nascent
reason allowed it to conceive them.   Then the
first megalithic blocks were erected; then began
that mad heaping up and up, which was to last
nearly fifty centuries; and temples were built
above temples, palaces over palaces, each generation striving to outdo its predecessor by a more
titanic grandeur.

Afterwards, four thousand years ago, Thebes

was in the height of her glory, encumbered with gods and with magnificence, the focus of the light of the world in the most ancient historic periods; while our Occident was still asleep and Greece and Assyria were scarcely awakened. Only in the extreme East, a humanity of a different race, the yellow people, called to follow in totally different ways, was fixing, so that they remain even to our day, the oblique lines of its angular roofs and the rictus of its monsters.

The men of Thebes, if they still saw too massively and too vastly, at least saw straight; they saw calmly, at the same time as they saw for ever. Their conceptions, which had begun to inspire those of Greece, were afterwards in some measure to inspire our own. In religion, in art, in beauty under all its aspects, they were as much our ancestors as were the Aryans.

Later again, sixteen hundred years before the birth of Christ, in one of the apogees of the town which, in the course of its interminable duration, experienced so many fluctuations, some ostentatious kings thought fit to build on this ground, already covered with temples, that which still remains the most arresting marvel of the ruins: the hypostyle hall, dedicated to the God Amen, with its forest of columns, as monstrous as the trunk of the baobab and as high as towers, compared with which the pillars of our cathedrals are utterly insignificant. In those days the same gods reigned at Thebes as three thousand years before, but in the interval they had been transformed little by little in accordance with the progressive development of human thought, and Amen, the host of this prodigious hall, asserted himself more and more as the sovereign master of life and eternity. Pharaonic Egypt was really tending, in spite of some revolts, towards the notion of a divine unity; even, one might say, to the notion of a supreme pity, for she already had her Apis, emanating from the All-Powerful, born of a virgin mother, and come humbly to the earth in order to make acquaintance with suffering.

After Seti I. and the Ramses had built, in honour of Amen, this temple, which, beyond all doubt, is the grandest and most durable in the world, men still continued for another fifteen centuries to heap up in its neighbourhood those blocks of granite and marble and sandstone, whose enormity now amazes us. Even for the invaders of Egypt, the Greeks and Romans, this old ancestral town of towns remained imposing and unique. They repaired its ruins, and built here temple after temple, in a style which hardly ever changed. Even in the ages of decadence everything that raised itself from the old, sacred soil, seemed to be impregnated a little with the ancient grandeur.

And it was only when the early Christians ruled here, and after them the Moslem iconoclasts, that the destruction became final. To these new believers, who, in their simplicity, imagined themselves to be possessed of the ultimate religious formula, and to know by His right name the Great Unknowable, Thebes became the haunt of " false gods," the abomination of abominations, which it behoved them to destroy.

And so they set to work, penetrating with an ever-present fear into the profound depths of the gloomy sanctuaries, mutilating first of all the thousands of visages whose disconcerting smile frightened them, and then exhausting themselves in the effort to uproot the colossi, which, even with the help of levers, they could not move. It was no easy task indeed, for everything was as solid as geological masses, as rocks or promontories. But for five or six hundred years the town was given over to the caprice of desecrators.

And then came the centuries of silence and oblivion under the shroud of the desert sands, which, thickening each year, proceeded to bury, and, in the event, to preserve for us, this peerless relic.

And now, at last, Thebes is being exhumed and restored to a semblance of life—now, after a cycle of seven or eight thousand years, when our

Western humanity, having left the primitive gods
that we see here, to embrace the Christian conception, which, even yesterday, made it live, is
in way of denying everything, and struggles
before the enigma of death in an obscurity more
dismal and more fearful than in the commencement of the ages. (More dismal and more
fearful still in this, that the plea of youth is
gone.) From all parts of Europe curious and
unquiet spirits, as well as mere idlers, turn their
steps towards Thebes, the ancient mother. Men
clear the rubbish from its remains, devise ways
of retarding the enormous fallings of its ruins,
and dig in its old soil, stored with hidden
treasure.

And this evening on one of the portals to
which I have just mounted—that which opens
at the north-west and terminates the colossal
artery of temples and palaces, many very diverse
groups have already taken their places, after the
pilgrimage of the day amongst the ruins. And
others are hastening towards the staircase by
which we have just climbed, so as not to miss
the grand spectacle of the sun setting, always
with the same serenity, the same unchanging
magnificence, behind the town which once was
consecrated to it.

French, German, English: I see them below,
a lot of pygmy figures, issuing from the hypo-

style hall, and making their way towards us.
Mean and pitiful they look in their twentieth-
century travellers' costumes, hurrying along that
avenue where once defiled so many processions of
gods and goddesses. And yet this, perhaps, is
the only occasion on which one of these bands of
tourists does not seem to me altogether ridiculous. Amongst these groups of unknown people,
there is none who is not collected and thoughtful,
or who does not at least pretend to be so; and
there is some saving quality of grace, even some
grandeur of humility, in the sentiment which has
brought them to this town of Amen, and in the
homage of their silence.

We are so high on this portal that we might
fancy ourselves upon a tower, and the defaced
stones of which it is built are immeasurably large.
Instinctively each one sits with his face to the
glowing sun, and consequently to the outspread
distances of the fields and the desert.

Before us, under our feet, an avenue stretches
away, prolonging towards the fields the pomp of
the dead city—an avenue bordered by monstrous
rams, larger than buffaloes, all crouched on their
pedestals in two parallel rows in the traditional
hieratic pose. The avenue terminates beyond at
a kind of wharf or landing-stage which formerly
gave on to the Nile. It was there that the God
Amen, carried and followed by long trains of

priests, came every year to take his golden barge for a solemn procession. But it leads to-day only to the cornfields, for, in the course of successive centuries, the river has receded little by little and now winds its course a thousand yards away in the direction of Libya.

We can see, beyond, the old sacred Nile between the clusters of palm-trees on its banks; meandering there like a rosy pathway, which remains, nevertheless, in this hour of universal incandescence, astonishingly pale, and gleams occasionally with a bluish light. And on the farther bank, from one end to the other of the western horizon, stretches the chain of the Libyan mountains behind which the sun is about to plunge: a chain of red sandstone, parched since the beginning of the world—without a rival in the preservation to perpetuity of dead bodies—which the Thebans perforated to its extreme depths to fill it with sarcophagi.

We watch the sun descend. But we turn also to see, behind us, the ruins in this the traditional moment of their apotheosis. Thebes, the immense town-mummy, seems all at once to be ablaze—as if its old stones were able still to burn; all its blocks, fallen or upright, appear to have been suddenly made ruddy by the glow of fire.

On this side, too, the view embraces great peaceful distances. Past the last pylons, and

beyond the crumbling ramparts the country,
down there behind the town, presents the same
appearance as that we were facing a moment
before. The same cornfields, the same woods of
date-trees, that make a girdle of green palms
around the ruins. And, right in the background,
a chain of mountains is lit up and glows with a
vivid coral colour. It is the chain of the Arabian
desert, lying parallel to that of Libya, along the
whole length of the Nile Valley—which is thus
guarded on right and left by stones and sand
stretched out in profound solitudes.

In all the surrounding country which we
command from this spot there is no indication
of the present day; only here and there, amongst
the palm-trees, the villages of the field labourers,
whose houses of dried earth can scarcely have
changed since the days of the Pharaohs. Our
contemporary desecrators have up till now re-
spected the infinite desuetude of the place, and,
for the tourists who begin to haunt it, no one yet
has dared to build a hotel.

Slowly the sun descends; and behind us the
granites of the town-mummy seem to burn more
and more. It is true that a slight shadow of a
warmer tint, an amaranth violet, begins to en-
croach upon the lower parts, spreading along
the avenues and over the open spaces. But
everything that rises into the sky—the friezes

of the temples, the capitals of the columns, the sharp points of the obelisks—are still red as glowing embers. These all become imbued with light and continue to glow and shed a rosy illumination until the end of the twilight.

It is a glorious hour, even for the old dust of Egypt, which fills the air eternally, without detracting at all from its wonderful clearness. It savours of spices, of the Bedouin, of the bitumen of the sarcophagus. And here now it is playing the *rôle* of those powders of different shades of gold which the Japanese use for the backgrounds of their lacquered landscapes. It reveals itself everywhere, close to and on the horizon, modifying at its pleasure the colour of things, and giving them a kind of metallic lustre. The phantasy of its changes is unimaginable. Even in the distances of the countryside, it is busy indicating by little trailing clouds of gold the smallest pathways traversed by the herds.

And now the disc of the God of Thebes has disappeared behind the Libyan mountains, after changing its light from red to yellow and from yellow to green.

And thereupon the tourists, judging that the display is over for the night, commence to descend and make ready for departure. Some in carriages, others on donkeys, they go to recruit themselves with the electricity and elegance of Luxor,

the neighbouring town (wines and spirits are
paid for as extras, and we dress for dinner). And
the dust condescends to mark their exodus also by
a last cloud of gold beneath the palm-trees of the
road.

An immediate solemnity succeeds to their departure. Above the mud houses of the fellah
villages rise slender columns of smoke, which are
of a periwinkle-blue in the midst of the still yellow
atmosphere. They tell of the humble life of these
little homesteads, subsisting here, where in the
backward of the ages were so many palaces and
splendours.

And the first bayings of the watchdogs an-
nounce already the vague uneasiness of the evenings around the ruins. There is no one now within
the mummy-town, which seems all at once to have
grown larger in the silence. Very quickly the
violet shadow covers it, all save the extreme points
of its obelisks, which keep still a little of their
rose-colour. The feeling comes over you that a
sovereign mystery has taken possession of the
town, as if some vague phantom things had just
passed into it.

THEBES BY NIGHT

CHAPTER XV

THE feeling, almost, that you have grown suddenly smaller by entering there, that you are
dwarfed to less than human size—to such an
extent do the proportions of these ruins seem to
crush you—and the illusion, also, that the light,
instead of being extinguished with the evening,
has only changed its colour, and become blue:
that is what one experiences on a clear Egyptian
night, in walking between the colonnades of the
great temple at Thebes.

The place is, moreover, so singular and so terrible that its mere name would at once cast a spell
upon the spirit, even if one were ignorant of the
place itself. The hypostyle of the temple of the
God Amen—that could be no other thing but
one. For this hall is unique in the world, in the
same way as the Grotto of Fingal and the Hima-
layas are unique.

.   .   .   .

To wander absolutely alone at night in Thebes
requires during the winter a certain amount of
stratagem and a knowledge of the routine of the

tourists. It is necessary, first of all, to choose a
night on which the moon rises late and then,
having entered before the close of the day, to
escape the notice of the Bedouin guards who shut
the gates at nightfall. Thus have I manœuvred
to-day, and undisturbed, watching from a hiding
place on high, I have waited with the patience of
a stone Osiris, till the grand transformation scene
of the setting of the sun was played out once
more upon the ruins. Thebes, which, during the
day, is almost animated by reason of the presence
of the visitors and the gangs of fellahs who, singing the while, are busy at the diggings and the
clearing away of the rubbish, has emptied itself
little by little, while the blue shadows were mounting from the base of the monstrous sanctuaries.
I watched the people moving in a long row, like
a trail of ants, towards the western gate between
the pylons of the Ptolemies, and the last of them
had disappeared before the rosy light died away
on the topmost points of the obelisks.

It seemed as if the silence and the night arrived together from beyond the Arabian desert,
advanced together across the plain, spreading
out like a rapid oil-stain; then gained the town
from east to west, and rose rapidly from the
ground to the very summits of the temples.
And this march of the darkness was infinitely
solemn.

For the first few moments, indeed, you might imagine that it was going to be an ordinary night such as we know in our climate, and a sense of uneasiness takes hold of you in the midst of this confusion of enormous stones, which in the darkness would become a quite inextricable maze. Oh! the horror of being lost in these ruins of Thebes and not being able to see! But in the event the air preserved its transparency to such a degree, and the stars began soon to scintillate so brightly that the surrounding things could be distinguished almost as well as in the daytime.

Indeed, now that the time of transition between the day and night has passed, the eyes grow accustomed to the strange, blue, persistent clearness so that you seem suddenly to have acquired the pupils of a cat; and the ultimate effect is merely as if you saw through a smoked glass which changed all the various shades of this reddish-coloured country into one uniform tint of blue.

Behold me then, for some two or three hours, alone among the temples of the Pharaohs. The tourists, whom the carriages and donkeys are at this moment taking back to the hotels of Luxor, will not return till very late, when the full moon will have risen and be shedding its clear light upon the ruins. My post, while I waited, was

high up among the ruins on the margin of the
sacred Lake of Osiris, the still and enclosed water
of which is astonishing in that it has remained
there for so many centuries. It still conceals,
no doubt, numberless treasures confided to it in
the days of slaughters and pillages, when the
armies of the Persian and Nubian kings forced
the thick, surrounding walls.

In a few minutes, thousands of stars appear at
the bottom of this water, reflecting symmetrically
the veritable ones which now scintillate everywhere in the heavens. A sudden cold spreads
over the town-mummy, whose stones, still warm
from their exposure to the sun, cool very rapidly
in this nocturnal blue which envelops them as in
a shroud. I am free to wander where I please
without risk of meeting anyone, and I begin to
descend by the steps made by the falling of the
granite blocks, which have formed on all sides
staircases as if for giants. On the overturned
surfaces, my hands encounter the deep, clear-
cut hollows of the hieroglyphs, and sometimes
of those inevitable people, carved in profile, who
raise their arms, all of them, and make signs to
one another. On arriving at the bottom I am
received by a row of statues with battered faces,
seated on thrones, and without hindrance of any
kind, and recognising everything in the blue
transparency which takes the place of day, I

come to the great avenue of the palaces of
Amen.

We have nothing on earth in the least degree
comparable to this avenue, which passive multitudes took nearly three thousand years to con-
struct, expending, century after century, their
innumerable energies in carrying these stones,
which our machines now could not move. And
the objective was always the same: to prolong
indefinitely the perspectives of pylons, colossi
and obelisks, continuing always this same artery
of temples and palaces in the direction of the
old Nile—while the latter, on the contrary,
receded slowly, from century to century, towards
Libya. It is here, and especially at night, that
you suffer the feeling of having been shrunken
to the size of a pygmy. All round you rise monoliths mighty as rocks. You have to take twenty
paces to pass the base of a single one of them.
They are placed quite close together, too close,
it seems, in view of their enormity and mass.
There is not enough air between them, and the
closeness of their juxtaposition disconcerts you
more, perhaps, even than their massiveness.

The avenue which I have followed in an east-
erly direction abuts on as disconcerting a chaos of
granite as exists in Thebes—the hall of the feasts
of Thothmes III. What kind of feasts were they,
that this king gave here, in this forest of thick-

set columns, beneath these ceilings, of which the smallest stone, if it fell, would crush twenty men? In places the friezes, the colonnades, which seem almost diaphanous in the air, are outlined still with a proud magnificence in unbroken alignment against the star-strewn sky. Elsewhere the destruction is bewildering; fragments of columns, entablatures, bas-reliefs lie about in indescribable confusion, like a lot of scattered wreckage after a world-wide tempest. For it was not enough that the hand of man should overturn these things. Tremblings of the earth, at different times, have also come to shake this Cyclops palace which threatened to be eternal. And all this—which represents such an excess of force, of movement, of impulsion, alike for its erection as for its overthrow—all this is tranquil this evening, oh! so tranquil, although toppling as if for an imminent downfall—tranquil for ever, one might say, congealed by the cold and by the night.

I was prepared for silence in such a place, but not for the sounds which I commence to hear. First of all an osprey sounds the prelude, above my head and so close to me that it holds me trembling throughout its long cry. Then other voices answer from the depths of the ruins, voices very diverse, but all sinister. Some are only able to mew on two long-drawn notes: some

yelp like jackals round a cemetery, and others
again imitate the sound of a steel spring slowly
unwinding itself.   And this concert comes always
from above.   Owls, ospreys, screech-owls, all the
different kinds of birds, with hooked beaks and
round eyes, and silken wings that enable them to
fly noiselessly, have their homes amongst the
granites massively upheld in the air; and they
are celebrating now, each after its own fashion,
the nocturnal festival.   Intermittent calls break
upon the air, and long-drawn infiinitely mournful
wailings, that sometimes swell and sometimes
seem to be strangled and end in a kind of sob.
And then, in spite of the sonority of the vast
straight walls, in spite of the echoes which prolong the cries, the silence obstinately returns.
Silence.   The silence after all and beyond all
doubt is the true master at this hour of this
kingdom at once colossal, motionless and blue—
a silence that seems to be infinite, because we
know that there is nothing around these ruins,
nothing but the line of the dead sands, the threshold of the deserts.

.   .   .   .

I retrace my steps towards the west in the
direction of the hypostyle, traversing again the
avenue of monstrous splendours, imprisoned and,
as it were, dwarfed between the rows of sovereign
stones.   There are obelisks there, some upright,

some overthrown. One like those of Luxor, but much higher, remains intact and raises its sharp point into the sky; others, less well known in their exquisite simplicity, are quite plain and straight from base to summit, bearing only in relief gigantic lotus flowers, whose long climbing stems bloom above in the half light cast by the stars. The passage becomes narrower and more obscure, and it is necessary sometimes to grope my way. And then again my hands encounter the everlasting hieroglyphs carved everywhere, and sometimes the legs of a colossus seated on its throne. The stones are still slightly warm, so fierce has been the heat of the sun during the day. And certain of the granites, so hard that our steel chisels could not cut them, have kept their polish despite the lapse of centuries, and my fingers slip in touching them.

There is now no sound. The music of the night birds has ceased. I listen in vain—so attentively that I can hear the beating of my heart. Not a sound, not even the buzzing of a fly. Everything is silent, everything is ghostly; and in spite of the persistent warmth of the stones the air grows colder and colder, and one gets the impression that everything here is frozen—definitively—as in the coldness of death.

A vast silence reigns, a silence that has sub-

sisted for centuries, on this same spot, where
formerly for three or four thousand years rose
such an uproar of living men. To think of the
clamorous multitudes who once assembled here,
of their cries of triumph and anguish, of their
dying agonies! First of all the pantings of those
thousands of harnessed workers, exhausting themselves generation after generation, under the
burning sun, in dragging and placing one above
the other these stones, whose enormity now
amazes us. And the prodigious feasts, the music
of the long harps, the blares of the brazen trum-
pets; the slaughters and battles when Thebes
was the great and unique capital of the world,
an object of fear and envy to the kings of the
barbarian peoples who commenced to awake in
neighbouring lands; the symphonies of siege
and pillage, in days when men bellowed with
the throats of beasts. To think of all this, here
on this ground, on a night so calm and blue!
And these same walls of granite from Syene, on
which my puny hands now rest, to think of the
beings who have touched them in passing, who
have fallen by their side in last sanguinary con-
flicts, without rubbing even the polish from their
changeless surfaces!

.   .   .   .

I now arrive at the hypostyle of the temple
of Amen, and a sensation of fear makes me

hesitate at first on the threshold. To find himself in the dead of night before such a place might well make a man falter. It seems like some hall for Titans, a remnant of fabulous ages, which has maintained itself, during its long duration, by force of its very massiveness, like the mountains. Nothing human is so vast. Nowhere on earth have men conceived such dwellings. Columns after columns, higher and more massive than towers, follow one another so closely, in an excess of accumulation, that they produce a feeling almost of suffocation. They mount into the clear sky and sustain there traverses of stone which you scarcely dare to contemplate. One hesitates to advance; a feeling comes over you that you are become infinitesimally small and as easy to crush as an insect. The silence grows preternaturally solemn. The stars through all the gaps in the fearful ceilings seem to send their scintillations to you in an abyss. It is cold and clear and blue.

The central bay of this hypostyle is in the same line as the road I have been following since I left the hall of Thothmes. It prolongs and magnifies as in an apotheosis that same long avenue, for the gods and kings, which was the glory of Thebes, and which in the succession of the ages nothing has contrived to equal. The

columns which border it are so gigantic [1] that
their tops, formed of mysterious full-blown
petals, high up above the ground on which we
crawl, are completely bathed in the diffuse clearness of the sky. And enclosing this kind of
nave on either side, like a terrible forest, is
another mass of columns—monster columns, of
an earlier style, of which the capitals close
instead of opening, imitating the buds of some
flower which will never blossom. Sixty to the
right, sixty to the left, too close together for
their size, they grow thick like a forest of
baobabs that wanted space: they induce a feeling of oppression without possible deliverance,
of massive and mournful eternity.

And this, forsooth, was the place that I had
wished to traverse alone, without even the
Bedouin guard, who at night believes it his duty
to follow the visitors. But now it grows lighter
and lighter. Too light even, for a blue phosphorescence, coming from the eastern horizon, begins
to filter through the opacity of the colonnades
on the right, outlines the monstrous shafts, and
details them by vague glimmerings on their
edges. The full moon is risen, alas! and my hours
of solitude are nearly over.

.   .   .   .

[1] About thirty feet in circumference and seventy-five feet in
height including the capital.

The moon! Suddenly the stones of the summit, the copings, the formidable friezes, are lighted by rays of clear light, and here and there, on the bas-reliefs encircling the pillars, appear luminous trails which reveal the gods and goddesses engraved in the stone. They were watching in myriads around me, as I knew well, —coifed, all of them, in discs or great horns. They stare at one another with their arms raised, spreading out their long figures in an eager attempt at conversation. They are numberless, these eternally gesticulating gods. Wherever you look their forms are multiplied with a stupefying repetition. They seem to have some mysterious secret to convey to one another, but have perforce to remain silent, and for all the expressiveness of their attitudes their hands do not move. And hieroglyphs, too, repeated to infinity, envelop you on all sides like a multiple woof of mystery.

.   .   .   .

Minute by minute now, everything amongst these rigid dead things grows more precise. Cold, hard rays penetrate through the immense ruin, separating with a sharp incisiveness the light from the shadows. The feeling that these stones, wearied as they were with their long duration, might still be thoughtful, still mindful of their past, grows less—less than it was a few

moments before, far less than during the preceding blue phantasmagoria. Under this clear,
pale light, as in the daytime under the fire
of the sun, Thebes has lost for the moment
whatever remained to it of soul; it has receded farther into the backward of time, and
appears now nothing more than a vast gigantic
fossil that excites only our wonder and our
fear.

.   .   .   .

But the tourists will soon be here, attracted
by the moon. A league away, in the hotels
of Luxor, I can fancy how they have hurried
away from the tables, for fear of missing the
celebrated spectacle. For me, therefore, it is
time to beat a retreat, and, by the great avenue
again, I direct my steps towards the pylons of
the Ptolemies, where the night guards are
waiting.

They are busy already, these Bedouins, in
opening the gates for some tourists, who have
shown their permits, and who carry Kodaks,
magnesium to light up the temples—quite an
outfit in short.

Farther on, when I have taken the road to
Luxor, it is not long before I meet, under the
palm-trees and on the sands, the crowd, the main
body of the arrivals—some in carriages, some
on horseback, some on donkeys. There is a

noise of voices speaking all sorts of non-Egyptian languages. One is tempted to ask: " What is happening? A ball, a holiday, a grand marriage?" No. The moon is full to-night at Thebes, upon the ruins. That is all.

THEBES IN SUNLIGHT

CHAPTER XVI

It is two o'clock in the afternoon. A white angry fire pours from the sky, which is pale from excess of light. A sun inimical to the men of our climate scorches the enormous fossil which, crumbling in places, is all that remains of Thebes and which lies there like the carcass of a gigantic beast that has been dead for thousands of years, but is too massive ever to be annihilated.

In the hypostyle there is a little blue shade behind the monstrous pillars, but even that shade is dusty and hot. The columns too are hot, and so are all the blocks—and yet it is winter and the nights are cold, even to the point of frost. Heat and dust; a reddish dust, which hangs like an eternal cloud over these ruins of Upper Egypt, exhaling an odour of spices and mummy.

The great heat seems to augment the retrospective sensation of fatigue which seizes you as you regard these stones—too heavy for human strength—which are massed here in mountains. One almost seems to participate in the efforts, the exhaustions and the sweating toils of that people, with their muscles of brand new steel,

223

who in the carrying and piling of such masses
had to bear the yoke for thirty centuries.

Even the stones themselves tell of fatigue—
the fatigue of being crushed by one another's
weight for thousands of years; the suffering that
comes of having been too exactly carved, and
too nicely placed one above the other, so that
they seem to be riveted together by the force of
their mere weight. Oh! the poor stones of the
base that bear the weight of these awful pilings!

And the ardent colour of these things surprises
you. It has persisted. On the red sandstone of
the hypostyle, the paintings of more than three
thousand years ago are still to be seen; especially
above the central chamber, almost in the sky,
the capitals, in the form of great flowers, have
kept the lapis blues, the greens and yellows
with which their strange petals were long ago
bespeckled.

Decrepitude and crumbling and dust. In
broad daylight, under the magnificent splendour
of the life-giving sun, one realises clearly that all
here is dead, and dead since days which the
imagination is scarcely able to conceive. And
the ruin appears utterly irreparable. Here and
there are a few impotent and almost infantine
attempts at reparation, undertaken in the ancient
epochs of history by the Greeks and Romans.
Columns have been put together, holes have been

filled with cement. But the great blocks lie in
confusion, and one feels, even to the point of
despair, how impossible it is ever to restore to
order such a chaos of crushing, overthrown things
—even with the help of legions of workers and
machines, and with centuries before you in which
to complete the task.

And then, what surprises and oppresses you
is the want of clear space, the little room that
remained for the multitudes in these halls which
are nevertheless immense. The whole space
between the walls was encumbered with pillars.
The temples were half filled with colossal forests
of stone. The men who built Thebes lived in the
beginning of time, and had not yet discovered
the thing which to us to-day seems so simple—
namely, the vault. And yet they were marvellous pioneers, these architects. They had already succeeded in evolving out of the dark, as
it were, a number of conceptions which, from
the beginning no doubt, slumbered in mysterious
germ in the human brain—the idea of rectitude,
the straight line, the right angle, the vertical
line, of which Nature furnishes no example, even
symmetry, which, if you consider it well, is less
explicable still. They employed symmetry with
a consummate mastery, understanding as well as
we do all the effect that is to be obtained by the
repetition of like objects placed *en pendant* on

either side of a portico or an avenue. But they
did not invent the vault. And therefore, since
there was a limit to the size of the stones which
they were able to place flat like beams, they had
recourse to this profusion of columns to support
their stupendous ceilings. And thus it is that
there seems to be a want of air, that one seems to
stifle in the middle of their temples, dominated
and obstructed as they are by the rigid presence
of so many stones. And yet to-day you can see
quite clearly in these temples, for, since the suspended rocks which served for roof have fallen,
floods of light descend from all parts. But
formerly, when a kind of half night reigned in
the deep halls, beneath the immovable carapaces
of sandstone or granite, how oppressive and
sepulchral it must all have been—how final and
pitiless, like a gigantic palace of Death! On one
day, however, in each year, here at Thebes, a light
as of a conflagration used to penetrate from one
end to the other of the sanctuaries of Amen; for
the middle artery is open towards the north-west,
and is aligned in such a fashion that, once a
year, one solitary time, on the evening of the
summer solstice, the sun as it sets is able to
plunge its reddened rays straight into the
sanctuaries. At the moment when it enlarges
its blood-coloured disc before descending behind the desolation of the Libyan mountains,

it arrives in the very axis of this avenue, of
this suite of aisles, which measures more than
800 yards in length.   Formerly, then, on these
evenings it shone horizontally beneath the terrible ceilings—between these rows of pillars which
are as high as our Colonne Vendôme—and threw,
for some seconds, its colours of molten copper into the obscurity of the holy of holies.
And then the whole temple would resound
with the clashing of music, and the glory of the
god of Thebes was celebrated in the depths of
the forbidden halls.

.   .   .   .

Like a cloud, like a veil, the continual red-
coloured dust floats everywhere above the ruins,
and, athwart it, here and there, the sun traces
long, white beams.   But at one point of the
avenue, behind the obelisks, it seems to rise in
clouds, this dust of Egypt, as if it were smoke.
For the workers of bronze are assembled there
to-day and, hour by hour, without ceasing, they
dig in the sacred soil.   Ridiculously small and
almost negligible by the side of the great
monoliths they dig and dig.   Patiently they
clear the ruins, and the earth goes away in little
parcels in rows of baskets carried by children in
the form of a chain.   The periodical deposits of
the Nile, and the sand carried by the wind of the
desert, had raised the soil by about six yards

since the time when Thebes ceased to live. But
now men are endeavouring to restore the ancient
level. At first sight the task seemed impossible,
but they will achieve it in the end, even with
their simple means, these fellah toilers, who sing
as they labour at their incessant work of ants.
Soon the grand hypostyle will be freed from
rubbish, and its columns, which even before
seemed so tremendous, uncovered now to the
base, have added another twenty feet to their
height. A number of colossal statues, which lay
asleep beneath this shroud of earth and sand,
have been brought back to the light, set upright
again and have resumed their watch in the
intimidating thoroughfares for a new period of
quasi-eternity. Year by year the town-mummy
is being slowly exhumed by dint of prodigious
effort; and is repeopled again by gods and kings
who had been hidden for thousands of years![1]
Year in, year out, the digging continues—deeper
and deeper. It is scarcely known to what depth
the debris and the ruins descend. Thebes had
endured for so many centuries, the earth here is
so penetrated with human past, that it is averred
that, under the oldest of the known temples,

[1] As is generally known, the maintenance of the ancient
monuments of Egypt and their restoration, so far as that may be
possible, has been entrusted to the French. M. Maspero has
delegated to Thebes an artist and a scholar, M. Legrain by
name, who is devoting his life passionately to the work.

there are still others, older still and more massive, of which there was no suspicion, and whose age must exceed eight thousand years.

In spite of the burning sun, and of the clouds of dust raised by the blows of the pickaxes, one might linger for hours amongst the dust-stained, meagre fellahs, watching the excavations in this unique soil—where everything that is revealed is by way of being a surprise and a lucky find, where the least carved stone had a past of glory, formed part of the first architectural splendours, was *a stone of Thebes*. Scarcely a moment passes but, at the bottom of the trenches, as the digging proceeds, some new thing gleams. Perhaps it is the polished flank of a colossus, fashioned out of granite from Syene, or a little copper Osiris, the debris of a vase, a golden trinket beyond price, or even a simple blue pearl that has fallen from the necklace of some waiting-maid of a queen.

This activity of the excavators, which alone reanimates certain quarters during the day, ends at sunset. Every evening the lean fellahs receive the daily wage of their labour, and take themselves off to sleep in the silent neighbourhood in their huts of mud; and the iron gates are shut behind them. At night, except for the guards at the entrance, no one inhabits the ruins.

.   .   .   .

Crumbling and dust. . . . Far around, on every
side of these palaces and temples of the central
artery—which are the best preserved and remain proudly upright—stretch great mournful
spaces, on which the sun from morning till
evening pours an implacable light.   There,
amongst the lank desert plants, lie blocks scattered at hazard—the remains of sanctuaries, of
which neither the plan nor the form will ever
be discovered.   But on these stones, fragments
of the history of the world are still to be read
in clear-cut hieroglyphs.

To the west of the hypostyle hall there is a
region strewn with discs, all equal and all alike.
It might be a draught-board for Titans with
draughts that would measure ten yards in circumference.   They are the scattered fragments,
slices, as it were, of a colonnade of the Ramses.
Farther on the ground seems to have passed
through fire.   You walk over blackish scoriæ en-
crusted with brazen bolts and particles of melted
glass.   It is the quarter burnt by the soldiers of
Cambyses.   They were great destroyers of the
queen city, were these same Persian soldiers.   To
break up the obelisks and the colossal statues they
conceived the plan of scorching them by lighting
bonfires around them, and then, when they saw
them burning hot, they deluged them with cold
water.   And the granites cracked from top to base.

It is well known, of course, that Thebes used to extend for a considerable distance both on this, the right, bank of the Nile, where the Pharaohs resided, and opposite, on the Libyan bank, given over to the preparers of mummies and to the mortuary temples. But to-day, except for the great palaces of the centre, it is little more than a litter of ruins, and the long avenues, lined with endless rows of sphinxes or rams, are lost, goodness knows where, buried beneath the sand.

At wide intervals, however, in the midst of these cemeteries of things, a temple here and there remains upright, preserving still its sanctified gloom beneath its cavernous carapace. One, where certain celebrated oracles used to be delivered, is even more prisonlike and sepulchral than the others in its eternal shadow. High up in a wall the black hole of a kind of grotto opens, to which a secret corridor coming from the depths used to lead. It was there that the face of the priest charged with the announcement of the sibylline words appeared—and the ceiling of his niche is all covered still with the smoke from the flame of his lamp, which was extinguished more than two thousand years ago!

.   .   .   .

What a number of ruins, scarcely emerging from the sand of the desert, are hereabout!

And in the old dried-up soil, how many strange
treasures remain hidden! When the sun lights
thus the forlorn distances, when you perceive
stretching away to the horizon these fields of
death, you realise better what kind of a place
this Thebes once was. Rebuilt as it were in the
imagination it appears excessive, superabundant
and multiple, like those flowers of the antediluvian
world which the fossils reveal to us. Compared
with it how our modern towns are dwarfed, and
our hasty little palaces, our stuccoes and old iron!

And it is so mystical, this town of Thebes,
with its dark sanctuaries, once inhabited by gods
and symbols. All the sublime, fresh-minded
striving of the human soul after the Unknowable
is as it were petrified in these ruins, in forms
diverse and immeasurably grand. And subsisting thus down to our day it puts us to shame.
Compared with this people, who thought only
of eternity, we are a lot of pitiful dotards, who
soon will be past caring about the wherefore
of life, or thought, or death. Such beginnings
presaged, surely, something greater than our
humanity of the present day, given over to despair, to alcohol and to explosives!

.   .   .   .

Crumbling and dust! This same sun of
Thebes is in its place each day, parching, exhausting, cracking and pulverising.

On the ground where once stood so much magnificence there are fields of corn, spread out like green carpets, which tell of the return of the humble life of tillage. Above all, there is the sand, encroaching now upon the very threshold of the Pharaohs; there is the yellow desert; there is the world of reflections and of silence, which approaches like a slow submerging tide. In the distance, where the mirage trembles from morning till evening, the burying is already almost achieved. The few poor stones which still appear, barely emerging from the advancing dunes, are the remains of what men, in their superb revolts against death, had contrived to make the most massively indestructible.

And this sun, this eternal sun, which parades over Thebes the irony of its duration—for us so impossible to calculate or to conceive! Nowhere so much as here does one suffer from the dismay of knowing that all our miserable little human effervescence is only a sort of fermentation round an atom emanated from that sinister ball of fire, and that that fire itself, the wonderful sun, is no more than an ephemeral meteor, a furtive spark, thrown off during one of the innumerable cosmic transformations, in the course of times without end and without beginning.

AN AUDIENCE OF
AMENOPHIS II.

CHAPTER XVII

KING AMENOPHIS II. has resumed his receptions, which he found himself obliged to suspend for three thousand, three hundred and some odd years, by reason of his decease. They are very well attended; court dress is not insisted upon, and the Grand Master of Ceremonies is not above taking a tip. He holds them every morning in the winter from eight o'clock, in the bowels of a mountain in the desert of Libya; and if he rests himself during the remainder of the day it is only because, as soon as midday sounds, they turn off the electric light.

Happy Amenophis! Out of so many kings who tried so hard to hide for ever their mummies in the depths of impenetrable caverns he is the only one who has been left in his tomb. And he "makes the most of it" every time he opens his funereal salons.

   .   .   .   .

It is important to arrive before midday at the dwelling of this Pharaoh, and at eight o'clock sharp, therefore, on a clear February morning, I set out from Luxor, where for many days my

dahabiya had slumbered against the bank of the
Nile.   It is necessary first of all to cross the
river, for the Theban kings of the Middle Empire
all established their eternal habitations on the
opposite bank—far beyond the plains of the
river shore, right away in those mountains which
bound the horizon as with a wall of adorable
rose-colour.   Other canoes, which are also crossing, glide by the side of mine on the tranquil
water.   The passengers seem to belong to that
variety of Anglo-Saxons which is equipped
by Thomas Cook & Son (Egypt Ltd.), and
like me, no doubt, they are bound for the royal
presence.

We land on the sand of the opposite bank,
which to-day is almost deserted.   Formerly there
stretched here a regular suburb of Thebes—
that, namely, of the preparers of mummies, with
thousands of ovens wherein to heat the natron
and the oils, which preserved the bodies from
corruption.   In this Thebes, where, for some fifty
centuries, everything that died, whether man or
beast, was minutely prepared and swathed in
bandages, it will readily be understood what
importance this quarter of the embalmers came
to assume.   And it was to the neighbouring
mountains that the products of so many careful
wrappings were borne for burial, while the Nile
carried away the blood from the bodies and the

filth of their entrails. That chain of living rocks
that rises before us, coloured each morning with
the same rose, as of a tender flower, is literally
stuffed with dead bodies.

We have to cross a wide plain before reaching
the mountains, and on our way cornfields alternate with stretches of sand already desertlike.
Behind us extends the old Nile and the opposite
bank which we have lately quitted—the bank of
Luxor, whose gigantic Pharaonic colonnades are
as it were lengthened below by their own reflection in the mirror of the river. And in this
radiant morning, in this pure light, it would be
admirable, this eternal temple, with its image
reversed in the depth of the blue water, were it
not that at its sides, and to twice its height, rises
the impudent Winter Palace, that monster hotel
built last year for the fastidious tourists. And
yet, who knows? The jackanapes who deposited
this abomination on the sacred soil of Egypt
perhaps imagines that he equals the merit of the
artist who is now restoring the sanctuaries of
Thebes, or even the glory of the Pharaohs who
built them.

As we draw nearer to the chain of Libya,
where this king awaits us, we traverse fields still
green with growing corn—and sparrows and
larks sing around us in the impetuous spring of
this land of Thebes.

And now beyond two menhirs, as it were, become gradually distinct. Of the same height
and shape, alike indeed in every respect, they
rise side by side in the clear distance in the
midst of these green plains, which recall so well
our fields of France. They wear the headgear
of the Sphinx, and are gigantic human forms
seated on thrones—the colossal statues of Memnon. We recognise them at once, for the picture-
makers of succeeding ages have popularised their
aspect, as in the case of the pyramids. What is
strange is that they should stand there so simply
in the midst of these fields of growing corn, which
reach to their very feet, and be surrounded by
these humble birds we know so well, who sing
without ceremony on their shoulders.

They do not seem to be scandalised even at
seeing now, passing quite close to them, the trucks
of a playful little railway belonging to a local
industry, that are laden with sugar-canes and
gourds.

The chain of Libya, during the last hour, has
been growing gradually larger against the profound and excessively blue sky. And now that
it rises up quite near to us, overheated, and as it
were incandescent, under this ten o'clock sun, we
begin to see on all sides, in front of the first rocky
spurs of the mountains, the debris of palaces, colonnades, staircases and pylons. Headless giants,

swathed like dead Pharaohs, stand upright, with hands crossed beneath their shroud of sandstone. They are the temples and statues for the manes of numberless kings and queens, who during three or four thousand years had their mummies buried hard by in the heart of the mountains, in the deepest of the walled and secret galleries.

And now the cornfields have ceased; there is no longer any herbage—nothing. We have crossed the desolate threshold, we are in the desert, and tread suddenly upon a disquieting funereal soil, half sand, half ashes, that is pitted on all sides with gaping holes. It looks like some region that had long been undermined by burrowing beasts. But it is men who, for more than fifty centuries, have vexed this ground, first to hide the mummies in it, and afterwards, and until our day, to exhume them. Each of these holes has enclosed its corpse, and if you peer within you may see yellow-coloured rags still trailing there; and bandages, or legs and vertebræ of thousands of years ago. Some lean Bedouins, who exercise the office of excavators, and sleep hard by in holes like jackals, advance to sell us scarabæi, blue-glass trinkets that are half fossilised, and feet or hands of the dead.

And now farewell to the fresh morning. Every minute the heat becomes more oppressive. The pathway that is marked only by a

row of stones turns at last and leads into the
depths of the mountain by a tragical passage.
We enter now into that " Valley of the Kings "
which was the place of the last rendezvous of
the most august mummies. The breaths of air
that reach us between these rocks are become
suddenly burning, and the site seems to belong
no longer to earth but to some calcined planet
which had for ever lost its clouds and atmosphere. This Libyan chain, in the distance so
delicately rose, is positively frightful now that it
overhangs us. It looks what it is—an enormous
and fantastic tomb, a natural necropolis, whose
vastness and horror nothing human could equal,
an ideal stove for corpses that wanted to endure
for ever. The limestone, on which for that
matter no rain ever falls from the changeless
sky, looks to be in one single piece from summit
to base, and betrays no crack or crevice by which
anything might penetrate into the sepulchres
within. The dead could sleep, therefore, in the
heart of these monstrous blocks as sheltered as
under vaults of lead. And of what there is of
magnificence the centuries have taken care. The
continual passage of winds laden with dust has
scaled and worn away the face of the rocks, so
as to leave only the denser veins of stone,
and thus have reappeared strange architectural
fantasies such as Matter, in the beginning, might

have dimly conceived. Subsequently the sun of Egypt has lavished on the whole its ardent reddish patines. And now the mountains imitate in places great organ-pipes, badigeoned with yellow and carmine, and elsewhere huge bloodstained skeletons and masses of dead flesh.

Outlined upon the excessive blue of the sky, the summits, illumined to the point of dazzling, rise up in the light—like red cinders of a glowing fire, splendours of living coal, against the pure indigo that turns almost to darkness. We seem to be walking in some valley of the Apocalypse with flaming walls. Silence and death, beneath a transcendent clearness, in the constant radiance of a kind of mournful apotheosis—it was such surroundings as these that the Egyptians chose for their necropoles.

The pathway plunges deeper and deeper into the stifling defiles, and at the end of this " Valley of the Kings," under this sun now nearly meridian, which grows each minute more mournful and terrible, we expected to come upon a dread silence. But what is this?

At a turning, beyond there, at the bottom of a sinister-looking recess, what does this crowd of people, what does this uproar mean? Is it a meeting, a fair? Under awnings to protect them from the sun stand some fifty donkeys, saddled in the English fashion. In a corner an electrical

workshop, built of new bricks, shoots forth its
black smoke, and all about, between the high,
blood-coloured walls, coming and going, making
a great stir and gabbling to their hearts' content,
are a number of Cook's tourists of both sexes, and
some even who verily seem to have no sex at all.
They are come for the royal audience; some on
asses, some in jaunting cars, and some, the stout
ladies who are grown short of wind, in chairs
carried by the Bedouins. From the four points
of Europe they have assembled in this desert
ravine to see an old dried-up corpse at the bottom
of a hole.

Here and there the hidden palaces reveal their
dark, square-shaped entrances, hewn in the
massive rock, and over each a board indicates
the name of a kingly mummy—Ramses IV.,
Seti I., Thothmes III., Ramses IX., etc. Although all these kings, except Amenophis II.,
have recently been removed and carried away to
Lower Egypt, to people the glass cases of the
museum of Cairo, their last dwellings have not
ceased to attract crowds. From each underground habitation are emerging now a number
of perspiring Cooks and Cookesses. And from
that of Amenophis, especially, they issue rapidly.
Suppose that we have come too late and that the
audience is over!

And to think that these entrances had been

walled up, had been masked with so much care, and lost for centuries! And of all the persever- ance that was needed to discover them, the ob- servation, the gropings, the soundings and ran- dom discoveries!

But now they are being closed. We loitered too long around the colossi of Memnon and the palaces of the plain. It is nearly noon, a noon consuming and mournful, which falls perpendic- ularly upon the red summits, and is burning to its deepest recesses the valley of stone.

At the door of Amenophis we have to cajole, beseech. By the help of a gratuity the Bedouin Grand Master of Ceremonies allows himself to be persuaded. We are to descend with him, but quickly, quickly, for the electric light will soon be extinguished. It will be a short audience, but at least it will be a private one. We shall be alone with the king.

In the darkness, where at first, after so much sunlight, the little electric lamps seem to us scarcely more than glow-worms, we expected a certain amount of chilliness as in the undergrounds of our climate. But here there is only a more oppressive heat, stifling and withering, and we long to re- turn to the open air, which was burning indeed, but was at least the air of life.

Hastily we descend: by steep staircases, by passages which slope so rapidly that they hurry

us along of themselves, like slides; and it
seems that we shall never ascend again, any
more than the great mummy who passed here
so long ago on his way to his eternal chamber.
All this brings us, first of all, to a deep well—
dug there to swallow up the desecrators in their
passage—and it is on one of the sides of this
oubliette, behind a casual stone carefully sealed,
that the continuation of these funeral galleries
was discovered. Then, when we have passed
the well, by a narrow bridge that has been thrown
across it, the stairs begin again, and the steep
passages that almost make you run; but now,
by a sharp bend, they have changed their direction. And still we descend, descend. Heavens!
how deep down this king dwells! And at each
step of our descent we feel more and more
imprisoned under the sovereign mass of stone,
in the centre of all this compact and silent
thickness.

.   .   .   .

The little electric globes, placed apart like a
garland, suffice now for our eyes which have
forgotten the sun. And we can distinguish
around us myriad figures inviting us to solemnity
and silence. They are inscribed everywhere on
the smooth, spotless walls of the colour of old
ivory. They follow one another in regular order,
repeating themselves obstinately in parallel rows,

as if the better to impose upon our spirit, with gestures and symbols that are eternally the same. The gods and demons, the representations of Anubis, with his black jackal's head and his long, erect ears, seem to make signs to us with their long arms and long fingers: " No noise! Look, there are mummies here!" The wonderful preservation of all this, the vivid colours, the clearness of the outlines, begin to cause a kind of stupor and bewilderment. Verily you would think that the painter of these figures of the shades had only just quitted the hypogeum. All this past seems to draw you to itself like an abyss to which you have approached too closely. It surrounds you, and little by little masters you. It is so much at home here that it has *remained the present.* Over and above the mere descent into the secret bowels of the rock there has been a kind of seizure with vertigo, which we had not anticipated and which has whirled us far away into the depths of the ages.

These interminable, oppressive passages, by which we have crawled to the innermost depths of the mountain, lead at length to something vast, the walls divide, the vault expands and we are in the great funeral hall, of which the blue ceiling, all bestrewn with stars like the sky, is supported by six pillars hewn in the rock itself. On either side open other chambers into which the electricity permits us to see quite clearly, and opposite, at the end of the hall, a large crypt is revealed, which one divines instinctively must be the resting place of the Pharaoh. What a prodigious labour must have been entailed by this perforation of the living rock! And this hypogeum is not unique. All along the " Valley of the Kings " little insignificant doors—which to the initiated reveal the " Sign of the Shadow," inscribed on their lintels—lead to other subterranean places, just as sumptuous and perfidiously profound, with their snares, their hidden wells, their oubliettes and the bewildering multiplicity of their mural figures. And all these tombs this morning were full of people, and, if we had not had the good fortune to arrive after the usual hour, we should have met here, even in this dwelling of Amenophis, a battalion equipped by Messrs Cook.

In this hall, with its blue ceiling, the frescoes multiply their riddles: scenes from the Book of Hades, all the funeral ritual translated into pictures. On the pillars and walls crowd the different demons that an Egyptian soul was likely to meet in its passage through the country of shadows, and underneath the passwords which were to be given to each of them are recapitulated so as not to be forgotten.

For the soul used to depart simultaneously

under the two forms of a flame [1] and a falcon [2] respectively. And this country of shadows, called also the west, to which it had to render itself, was that where the moon sinks and where each evening the sun goes down; a country to which the living were never able to attain, because it fled before them, however fast they might travel across the sands or over the waters. On its arrival there, the scared soul had to parley successively with the fearsome demons who lay in wait for it along its route. If at last it was judged worthy to approach Osiris, the great Dead Sun, it was subsumed in him and reappeared, shining over the world the next morning and on all succeeding mornings until the consummation of time—a vague survival in the solar splendour, a continuation without personality, of which one is scarcely able to say whether or not it was more desirable than eternal nonexistence.

And, moreover, it was necessary to preserve the body at whatever cost, for a certain *double* of the dead man continued to dwell in the dry flesh, and retained a kind of half life, barely conscious. Lying at the bottom of the sarcophagus it was able to see, by virtue of those two eyes, which were painted on the lid, always in

[1] The Khou, which never returned to our world.

[2] The Bai, which might, at its will, revisit the tomb.

the same axis as the empty eyes of the mummy. Sometimes, too, this *double,* escaping from the mummy and its box, used to wander like a phantom about the hypogeum. And, in order that at such times it might be able to obtain nourishment, a mass of mummified viands wrapped in bandages were amongst the thousand and one things buried at its side. Even natron and oils were left, so that it might re-embalm itself, if the worms came to life in its members.

Oh! the persistence of this *double,* sealed there in the tomb, a prey to anxiety lest corruption should take hold of it; which had to serve its long duration in suffocating darkness, in absolute silence, without anything to mark the days and nights, or the seasons or the centuries, or the tens of centuries without end! It was with such a terrible conception of death as this that each one in those days was absorbed in the preparation of his eternal chamber.

And for Amenophis II. this more or less is what happened to his *double.* Unaccustomed to any kind of noise, after three or four hundred years passed in the company of certain familiars, lulled in the same heavy slumber as himself, he heard the sound of muffled blows in the distance, by the side of the hidden well. The secret entrance was discovered: men were breaking through its walls! Living beings were about to appear, pillagers of tombs, no doubt, come to unswathe them all! But no! Only some priests of Osiris, advancing with fear in a funeral procession. They brought nine great coffins containing the mummies of nine kings, his sons, grandsons and other unknown successors, down to that King Setnakht, who governed Egypt two and a half centuries after him. It was simply to hide them better that they brought them hither, and placed them all together in a chamber that was immediately walled up. Then they departed. The stones of the door were sealed afresh, and everything fell again into the old mournful and burning darkness.

Slowly the centuries rolled on—perhaps ten, perhaps twenty—in a silence no longer even disturbed by the scratchings of the worms, long since dead. And a day came when, at the side of the entrance, the same blows were heard again. . . . And this time it was the robbers. Carrying torches in their hands, they rushed headlong in, with shouts and cries and, except in the safe hiding place of the nine coffins, everything was plundered, the bandages torn off, the golden trinkets snatched from the necks of the mummies. Then, when they had sorted their booty, they walled up the entrance as before, and went their way, leaving an inextricable confusion of shrouds, of human bodies, of entrails issuing from shattered vases, of broken gods and emblems.

Afterwards, for long centuries, there was silence again, and finally, in our days, the *double,* then in its last weakness and almost non-existent, perceived the same noise of stones being unsealed by blows of pickaxes. The third time, the living men who entered were of a race never seen before. At first they seemed respectful and pious, only touching things gently. But they came to plunder everything, even the nine coffins in their still inviolate hiding place. They gathered the smallest fragments with a solicitude almost religious. That they might lose nothing they even sifted the rubbish and the dust. But, as for Amenophis, who was already nothing more than a lamentable mummy, without jewels or bandages, they left him at the bottom of his sarcophagus of sandstone. And since that day, doomed to receive each morning numerous people of a strange aspect, he dwells alone in his hypogeum, where there is now neither a being nor a thing belonging to his time.

But yes, there is! We had not looked all round. There in one of the lateral chambers some bodies are lying, dead bodies—three corpses (unswathed at the time of the pillage), side by side on their rags. First, a woman, the queen probably, with loosened hair. Her profile has preserved its exquisite lines. How beautiful she still is! And then a young boy with the little greyish face of a doll. His head is shaved, except for that long curl at the right side, which denotes a prince of the royal blood. And the third a man. Ugh! how terrible he is—looking as if he found death a thing irresistibly comical. He even writhes with laughter, and eats a corner of his shroud as if to prevent himself from bursting into a too unseemly mirth.

And then, suddenly, black night! And we stand as if congealed in our place. The electric light has gone out—everywhere at once. Above, on the earth, midday must have sounded—for those who still have cognisance of the sun and the hours.

The guard who has brought us hither shouts in his Bedouin falsetto, in order to get the light switched on again, but the infinite thickness of the walls, instead of prolonging the vibrations, seems to deaden them; and besides, who could hear us, in the depths where we now are? Then, groping in the absolute darkness, he makes his way up the sloping passage. The hurried patter of his sandals and the flapping of his burnous grow faint in the distance, and the cries that he continues to utter sound so smothered to us soon that we might ourselves be buried. And meanwhile we do not move. But how comes it that it

is so hot amongst these mummies? It seems as
if there were fires burning in some oven close by.
And above all there is a want of air. Perhaps
the corridors, after our passage, have con-
tracted, as happens sometimes in the anguish
of dreams. Perhaps the long fissure by which
we have crawled hither, perhaps it has closed in
upon us. . . .

But at length the cries of alarm are heard and
the light is turned on again. The three corpses
have not profited by the unguarded moments to
attempt any aggress˙ _ movement. Their posi-
tions, their expressions have not changed: the
queen calm and beautiful as ever; the man eating
still the corner of his rags to stifle that mad
laughter of thirty-three centuries.

The Bedouin has now returned, breathless
from his journey. He urges us to come to see
the king before the electric light is again extinguished, and this time for good and all. Behold
us now at the end of the hall, on the edge of
a dark crypt, leaning over and peering within.
It is a place oval in form, with a vault of a
funereal black, relieved by frescoes, either white
or of the colour of ashes. They represent, these
frescoes, a whole new register of gods and
demons, some slim and sheathed narrowly like
mummies, others with big heads and big bellies
like hippopotami. Placed on the ground and

watched from above by all these figures is an enormous sarcophagus of stone, wide open; and in it we can distinguish vaguely the outline of a human body: the Pharaoh!

At least we should have liked to see him better. The necessary light is forthcoming at once: the Bedouin Grand Master of Ceremonies touches an electric button and a powerful lamp illumines the face of Amenophis, detailing with a clearness that almost frightens you the closed eyes, the grimacing countenance, and the whole of the sad mummy. This theatrical effect took us by surprise; we were not prepared for it.

He was buried in magnificence, but the pillagers have stripped him of everything, even of his beautiful breastplate of tortoiseshell, which came to him from a far-off Oriental country, and for many centuries now he has slept half naked on his rags. But his poor bouquet is there still —of mimosa, recognisable even now, and who will ever tell what pious or perhaps amorous hand it was that gathered these flowers for him, more than three thousand years ago.

The heat is suffocating. The whole crushing mass of this mountain, of this block of limestone, into which we have crawled through relatively imperceptible holes, like white ants or larvæ, seems to weigh upon our chest. And these figures too, inscribed on every side, and this mystery of the hieroglyphs and the symbols, cause a growing uneasiness. You are too near them, they seem too much the masters of the exits, these gods with their heads of falcon, ibis and jackal, who, on the walls, converse in a continual exalted pantomime. And then the feeling comes over you, that you are guilty of sacrilege standing there, before this open coffin, in this unwonted insolent light. The dolorous, blackish face, half eaten away, seems to ask for mercy: "Yes, yes, my sepulchre has been violated and I am returning to dust. But now that you have seen me, leave me, turn out that light, have pity on my nothingness."

In sooth, what a mockery! To have taken so many pains, to have adopted so many stratagems to hide his corpse; to have exhausted thousands of men in the hewing of this underground labyrinth, and to end thus, with his head in the glare of an electric lamp, to amuse whoever passes.

And out of pity—I think it was the poor bouquet of mimosa that awakened it—I say to the Bedouin: "Yes, put out the light, put it out—that is enough."

And then the darkness returns above the royal countenance, which is suddenly effaced in the sarcophagus. The phantom of the Pharaoh is vanished, as if replunged into the unfathomable past.   The audience is over.

And we, who are able to escape from the horror of the hypogeum, reascend rapidly towards the sunshine of the living, we go to breathe the air again, the air to which we have still a right —for some few days longer.

AT THEBES IN THE TEMPLE
OF THE OGRESS

CHAPTER XVIII

THIS evening, in the vast chaos of ruins—at the hour in which the light of the sun begins to turn to rose—I make my way along one of the magnificent roads of the town-mummy, that, in fact, which goes off at a right angle to the line of the temples of Amen, and, losing itself more or less in the sands, leads at length to a sacred lake on the border of which certain cat-headed goddesses are seated in state watching the dead water and the expanse of the desert. This particular road was begun three thousand four hundred years ago by a beautiful queen called Makeri,[1] and in the following centuries a number of kings continued its construction. It was ornamented with pylons of a superb massiveness—pylons are monumental walls, in the form of a trapezium with a wide base, covered entirely with hieroglyphs, which the Egyptians used to place at either side of their porticoes and long avenues—as well as by colossal statues and interminable rows of rams, larger than buffaloes, crouched on pedestals.

[1] To-day the mummy with the baby in the museum at Cairo.

At the first pylons I have to make a detour.
They are so ruinous that their blocks, fallen
down on all sides, have closed the passage. Here
used to watch, on right and left, two upright
giants of red granite from Syene. Long ago,
in times no longer precisely known, they were
broken off, both of them, at the height of the
loins. But their muscular legs have kept their
proud, marching attitude, and each in one of the
armless hands, which reach to the end of the
cloth that girds their loins, clenches passionately
the emblem of eternal life. And this Syenite
granite is so hard that time has not altered it in
the least; in the midst of the confusion of stones
the thighs of these mutilated giants gleam as if
they had been polished yesterday.

Farther on we come upon the second pylons,
foundered also, before which stands a row of
Pharaohs.

On every side the overthrown blocks display
their utter confusion of gigantic things in the
midst of the sand which continues patiently to
bury them. And here now are the third pylons,
flanked by their two marching giants, who have
neither head nor shoulders. And the road,
marked majestically still by the debris, continues
to lead towards the desert.

And then the fourth and last pylons, which
seem at first sight to mark the extremity of the

ruins, the beginning of the desert nothingness. Time-worn and uncrowned, but stiff and upright still, they seem to be set there so solidly that nothing could ever overthrow them. The two colossal statues which guard them on the right and left are seated on thrones. One, that on the eastern side, has almost disappeared. But the other stands out entire and white, with the whiteness of marble, against the brown-coloured background of the enormous stretch of wall covered with hieroglyphs. His face alone has been mutilated; and he preserves still his imperious chin, his ears, his Sphinx's headgear, one might almost say his meditative expression, before this deployment of the vast solitude which seems to begin at his very feet.

Here however was only the boundary of the quarters of the God Amen. The boundary of Thebes was much farther on, and the avenue which will lead me directly to the home of the cat-headed goddesses extends farther still to the old gates of the town; albeit you can scarcely distinguish it between the double row of Kriosphinxes all broken and well-nigh buried.

The day falls, and the dust of Egypt, in accordance with its invariable practice every evening, begins to resemble in the distance a powder of gold. I look behind me from time to time at the giant who watches me, seated at the foot of his pylon on which the history of a Pharaoh is carved in one immense picture. Above him and above his wall, which grows each minute more rose-coloured, I see, gradually mounting in proportion as I move away from it, the great mass of the palaces of the centre, the hypostyle hall, the halls of Thothmes and the obelisks, all the entangled cluster of those things at once so grand and so dead, which have never been equalled on earth.

And as I continue to gaze upon the ruins, resplendent now in the rosy apotheosis of the evening, they come to look like the crumbling remains of a gigantic skeleton. They seem to be begging for a merciful surcease, as if they were tired of this endless gala colouring at each setting of the sun, which mocks them with its eternity.

All this is now a long way behind me; but the air is so limpid, the outlines remain so clear that the illusion is rather that the temples and the pylons grow smaller, lower themselves and sink into the earth. The white giant who follows me always with his sightless stare is now reduced to the proportions of a simple human dreamer. His attitude moreover has not the rigid hieratic aspect of the other Theban statues. With his hands upon his knees he looks like a mere ordinary mortal who had stopped to

reflect.[1] I have known him for many days—for
many days and many nights, for, what with his
whiteness and the transparency of these Egyptian
nights, I have seen him often outlined in the distance under the dim light of the stars—a great
phantom in his contemplative pose. And I feel
myself obsessed now by the continuance of his
attitude at this entrance of the ruins—I who shall
pass without a morrow from Thebes and even
from the earth—even as we all pass. Before conscious life was vouchsafed to me he was there, had
been there since times which make you shudder
to think upon. For three and thirty centuries,
or thereabouts, the eyes of myriads of unknown
men and women, who have gone before me, saw
him just as I see him now, tranquil and white, in
this same place, seated before this same threshold,
with his head a little bent, and his pervading air
of thought.

I make my way without hastening, having
always a tendency to stop and look behind
me, to watch the silent heap of palaces and the
white dreamer, which now are all illumined
with a last Bengal fire in the daily setting of
the sun.

And the hour is already twilight when I reach
the goddesses.

Their domain is so destroyed that the sands

[1] Statue of Amenophis III.

had succeeded in covering and hiding it for centuries. But it has lately been exhumed.

There remain of it now only some fragments of columns, aligned in multiple rows in a vast extent of desert. Broken and fallen stones and debris.[1] I walk on without stopping, and at length reach the sacred lake on the margin of which the great cats are seated in eternal council, each one on her throne. The lake, dug by order of the Pharaohs, is in the form of an arc, like a kind of crescent. Some marsh birds, that are about to retire for the night, now traverse its mournful, sleeping water. Its borders, which have known the utmost of magnificence, are become mere heaps of ruins on which nothing grows. And what one sees beyond, what the attentive goddesses themselves regard, is the empty desolate plain, on which some few poor fields of corn mingle in this twilight hour with the sad infinitude of the sands. And the whole is bounded on the horizon by the chain, still a little rose-coloured, of the limestones of Arabia.

They are there, the cats, or, to speak more exactly, the lionesses, for cats would not have those short ears, or those cruel chins, thickened by tufts of beard. All of black granite, images of Sekhet (who was the Goddess of War, and in her hours the Goddess of Lust), they have the

[1] The temple of the Goddess Mut.

slender body of a woman, which makes more terrible the great feline head surmounted by its high
bonnet. Eight or ten, or perhaps more, they
are more disquieting in that they are so numerous
and so alike. They are not gigantic, as one might
have expected, but of ordinary human stature
—easy therefore to carry away, or to destroy,
and that again, if one reflects, augments the
singular impression they cause. When so many
colossal figures lie in pieces on the ground, how
comes it that they, little people seated so tran-
quilly on their chairs, have contrived to remain
intact, during the passing of the three and thirty
centuries of the world's history?

The passage of the marsh birds, which for a
moment disturbed the clear mirror of the lake,
has ceased. Around the goddesses nothing moves
and the customary infinite silence envelops them
as at the fall of every night. They dwell indeed
in such a forlorn corner of the ruins! Who, to
be sure, even in broad daylight, would think of
visiting them?

Down there in the west a trailing cloud of
dust indicates the departure of the tourists,
who had flocked to the temple of Amen, and now
hasten back to Luxor, to dine at the various
tables d'hôte. The ground here is so felted with
sand that in the distance we cannot hear the rolling of their carriages. But the knowledge that

they are gone renders more intimate the inter-
view with these numerous and identical goddesses,
who little by little have been draped in shadow.
Their seats turn their backs to the palaces of
Thebes, which now begin to be bathed in violet
waves and seem to sink towards the horizon, to
lose each minute something of their importance
before the sovereignty of the night.

And the black goddesses, with their lioness'
heads and tall headgear—seated there with their
hands upon their knees, with eyes fixed since the
beginning of the ages, and a disturbing smile on
their thick lips, like those of a wild beast—continue to regard—beyond the little dead lake—
that desert, which now is only a confused immensity, of a bluish ashy-grey. And the fancy
seizes you that they are possessed of a kind of
life, which has come to them after long waiting,
by virtue of that *expression* which they have worn
on their faces so long, oh! so long.

. . . .

Beyond, at the other extremity of the ruins,
there is a sister of these goddesses, taller than
they, a great Sekhet, whom in these parts men
call the Ogress, and who dwells alone and upright, ambushed in a narrow temple. Amongst
the fellahs and the Bedouins of the neighbourhood she enjoys a very bad reputation, it being
her custom of nights to issue from her temple,

and devour men; and none of them would willingly venture near her dwelling at this late hour. But instead of returning to Luxor, like the good people whose carriages have just departed, I rather choose to pay her a visit.

Her dwelling is some distance away, and I shall not reach it till the dead of night.

First of all I have to retrace my steps, to return along the whole avenue of rams, to pass again by the feet of the white giant, who has already assumed his phantomlike appearance, while the violet waves that bathed the town-mummy thicken and turn to a greyish-blue. And then, leaving behind me the pylons guarded by the broken giants, I thread my way among the palaces of the centre.

It is among these palaces that I encounter for good and all the night, with the first cries of the owls and ospreys. It is still warm there, on account of the heat stored by the stones during the day, but one feels nevertheless that the air is freezing.

At a crossing a tall human figure looms up, draped in black and armed with a baton. It is a roving Bedouin, one of the guards, and this more or less is the dialogue exchanged between us (freely and succinctly translated):

" Your permit, sir."

" Here it is."

(Here we combine our efforts to illuminate the said permit by the light of a match.)

" Good, I will go with you."

" No. I beg of you."

" Yes; I had better. Where are you go-ing? "

" Beyond, to the temple of that lady—you know, who is great and powerful and has a face like a lioness."

" Ah! . . . Yes, I think I understand that you would prefer to go alone." (Here the intonation becomes infantine.) " But you are a kind gentle-man and will not forget the poor Bedouin all the same."

He goes his way. On leaving the palaces I have still to traverse an extent of uncultivated country, where a veritable cold seizes me. Above my head no longer the heavy suspended stones, but the far-off expanse of the blue night sky—where are shining now myriads upon myriads of stars. For the Thebans of old this beautiful vault, scintillating always with its powder of diamonds, shed no doubt only serenity upon their souls. But for us, *who know, alas!* it is on the contrary the field of the great fear, which, out of pity, it would have been better if we had never been able to see; the incommensurable black void, where the worlds in their frenzied whirling precipitate themselves like rain, crash into and

annihilate one another, only to be renewed for
fresh eternities.

All this is seen too vividly, the horror of it becomes intolerable, on a clear night like this, in
a place so silent and littered so with ruins.   More
and more the cold penetrates you—the mournful
cold of the sidereal spheres from which nothing
now seems to protect you, so rarefied—almost
non-existent—does the limpid atmosphere appear.   And the gravel, the poor dried herbs, that
crackle under foot, give the illusion of the crunch-
ing noise we know at home on winter nights when
the frost is on the ground.

I approach at length the temple of the Ogress.
These stones which now appear, whitish in
the night, this secret-looking dwelling near the
boundary wall of Thebes, proclaim the spot, and
verily at such an hour as this it has an evil
aspect.   Ptolemaic columns, little vestibules, little courtyards where a dim blue light enables
you to find your way.   Nothing moves; not
even the flight of a night bird: an absolute
silence, magnified awfully by the presence of the
desert which you feel encompasses you beyond
these walls.   And beyond, at the bottom, three
chambers made of massive stone, each with its
separate entrance.   I know that the first two are
empty.   It is in the third the Ogress dwells,
unless, indeed, she have already set out upon her

nocturnal hunt for human flesh. Pitch darkness reigns within and I have to grope my way. Quickly I light a match. Yes, there she is indeed, alone and upright, almost part of the end wall, on which my little light makes the horrible shadow of her head dance. The match goes out —irreverently I light many more under her chin, under that heavy, man-eating jaw. In very sooth, she is terrifying. Of black granite—like her sisters, seated on the margin of the mournful lake—but much taller than they, from six to eight feet in height, she has a woman's body, exquisitely slim and young, with the breasts of a virgin. Very chaste in attitude, she holds in her hand a long-stemmed lotus flower, but by a contrast that nonplusses and paralyses you the delicate shoulders support the monstrosity of a huge lioness' head. The lappets of her bonnet fall on either side of her ears almost down to her breast, and surmounting the bonnet, by way of addition to the mysterious pomp, is a large moon disc. Her dead stare gives to the ferocity of her visage something unreasoning and fatal; an irresponsible ogress, without pity as without pleasure, devouring after the manner of Nature and of Time. And it was so perhaps that she was understood by the initiated of ancient Egypt, who symbolised everything for the people in the figures of gods.

In the dark retreat, enclosed with defaced stones, in the little temple where she stands, alone, upright and grand, with her enormous head and thrust-out chin and tall goddess' head-dress—one is necessarily quite close to her. In touching her, at night, you are astonished to find that she is less cold than the air; she becomes somebody, and the intolerable dead stare seems to weigh you down.

During the *tête-à-tête,* one thinks involuntarily of the surroundings, of these ruins in the desert, of the prevailing nothingness, of the cold beneath the stars. And, now, that summation of doubt and despair and terror, which such an assemblage of things inspires in you, is confirmed, if one may say so, by the meeting with this divinity-symbol, which awaits you at the end of the journey, to receive ironically all human prayer; a rigid horror of granite, with an implacable smile and a devouring jaw.

A TOWN PROMPTLY
EMBELLISHED

CHAPTER XIX

A TOWN PROMPTLY EMBELLISHED

EIGHT years and a line of railway have sufficed to accomplish its metamorphosis. Once in Upper Egypt, on the borders of Nubia, there was a little humble town, rarely visited, and wanting, it must be owned, in elegance and even in comfort.

Not that it was without picturesqueness and historical interest. Quite the contrary. The Nile, charged with the waters of equatorial Africa, flung itself close by from the height of a mass of black granite, in a majestic cataract; and then, before the little Arab houses, became suddenly calm again, and flowed between islets of fresh verdure where clusters of palm-trees swayed their plumes in the wind.

And around were a number of temples, of hypogea, of Roman ruins, of ruins of churches dating from the first centuries of Christianity. The ground was full of souvenirs of the great primitive civilisations. For the place, abandoned for ages and lulled in the folds of Islam under the guardianship of its white mosque, was once one of the centres of the life of the world.

And, moreover, in the adjoining desert, some three or four thousand years ago, the ancient history of the world had been written by the Pharaohs in immortal hieroglyphics—well-nigh everywhere, on the polished sides of the strange blocks of blue and red granite that lie scattered about the sands and look now like the forms of antediluvian monsters.

.   .   .   .

Yes, but it was necessary that all this should be co-ordinated, focused as it were, and above all rendered accessible to the delicate travellers of the Agencies. And to-day we have the pleasure of announcing that, from December to March, Assouan (for that is the name of the fortunate locality) has a " season " as fashionable as those of Ostend or Spa.

In approaching it, the huge hotels erected on all sides—even on the islets of the old river—charm the eye of the traveller, greeting him with their welcoming signs, which can be seen a league away. True, they have been somewhat hastily constructed, of mud and plaster, but they recall none the less those gracious palaces with which the Compagnie des Wagon-Lits has dowered the world. And how negligible now, how dwarfed by the height of their façades, is the poor little town of olden times, with its little houses, whitened with chalk, and its baby minaret.

The cataract, on the other hand, has disappeared from Assouan. The tutelary Albion wisely considered that it would be better to sacrifice that futile spectacle and, in order to increase the yield of the soil, to dam the waters of the Nile by an artificial barrage: a work of solid masonry which (in the words of the **Programme of Pleasure Trips**) " affords an interest of a very different nature and degree " (*sic*)'.

But nevertheless Cook & Son—a business concern glossed with poetry, as all the world knows —have endeavoured to perpetuate the memory of the cataract by giving its name to a hotel of 500 rooms, which as a result of their labours has been established opposite to those rocks— now reduced to silence—over which the old Nile used to seethe for so many centuries. " Cataract Hotel "—that gives the illusion still, does it not? —and looks remarkably well at the head of a sheet of notepaper.

Cook & Son (**Egypt Ltd.**) have even gone so far as to conceive the idea that it would be original to give to their establishment a certain *cachet* of Islam. And the dining-room reproduces (in imitation, of course—but then you must not expect the impossible) the interior of one of the mosques of Stamboul. At the luncheon hour it is one of the prettiest sights in the world to see, under this imitation holy cupola, all the little tables crowded with Cook's tourists of both sexes, the while a concealed orchestra strikes up the " Mattchiche."

The dam, it is true, in suppressing the cataract has raised some thirty feet or so the level of the water upstream, and by so doing has submerged a certain Isle of Philæ, which passed, absurdly enough, for one of the marvels of the world by reason of its great temple of Isis, surrounded by palm-trees. But between ourselves, one may say that the beautiful goddess was a little old-fashioned for our times. She and her mysteries had had their day. Besides, if there should be any chagrined soul who might regret the disappearance of the island, care has been taken to perpetuate the memory of it, in the same way as that of the cataract. Charming coloured postcards, taken before the submerging of the island and the sanctuary, are on sale in all the bookshops along the quay.

Oh! this quay of Assouan, already so British in its orderliness, its method! Nothing better cared for, nothing more altogether charming could be conceived. First of all there is the railway, which, passing between balustrades painted a grass-green, gives out its fascinating noise and joyous smoke. On one side is a row of hotels and shops, all European in character —hairdressers, perfumers, and numerous dark rooms for the use of the many amateur photographers, who make a point of taking away with them photographs of their travelling companions grouped tastefully before some celebrated hypogeum.

And then numerous *cafés,* where the whisky is of excellent quality. And, I ought to add, in justice to the result of the *Entente Cordiale,* you may see there, too, aligned in considerable quantities on the shelves, the products of those great French philanthropists, to whom indeed our generation does not render sufficient homage for all the good they have done to its stomach and its head. The reader will guess that I have named Pernod, Picon and Cusenier.

It may be indeed that the honest fellahs and Nubians of the neighbourhood, so sober a little while ago, are apt to abuse these tonics a little. But that is the effect of novelty, and will pass. And anyhow, amongst us Europeans, there is no need to conceal the fact—for do we not all make use of it involuntarily?—that alcoholism is a powerful auxiliary in the propagation of our ideas, and that the dealer in wines and spirits constitutes a valuable vanguard pioneer for our Western civilisation. Races, insensibly depressed by the abuse of our " appetisers," become more supple, more easy to lead in the true path of progress and liberty.

On this quay of Assouan, so carefully levelled, defiles briskly a continual stream of fair travellers ravishingly dressed as only those know how who have made a tour with Cook & Son (Egypt Ltd.). And along the Nile, in the shade of the young trees, planted with the utmost nicety and precision, the flower-beds and straight-cut turf are protected efficaciously by means of wire-netting against certain acts of forgetfulness to which dogs, alas, are only too much addicted.

Here, too, everything is ticketed, everything has its number: the donkeys, the donkey-drivers, the stations even where they are allowed to stand—" Stand for six donkeys, stand for ten, etc." Some very handsome camels, fitted with riding saddles, wait also in their respective places and a number of Cook ladies, meticulous on the point of local colour, even when it is merely a question of making some purchases in the town, readily mount for some moments one or other of these " ships of the desert."

And at every fifty yards a policeman, still Egyptian in his countenance, but quite English in his bearing and costume, keeps a vigilant eye on everything—would never suffer, for example, that an eleventh donkey should dare to take a place in a stand for ten, which was already full.

Certain people, inclined to be critical, might consider, perhaps, that these policemen were a

little too ready to chide their fellow-country-
men; whereas on the contrary they showed
themselves very respectful and obliging when-
ever they were addressed by a traveller in a
cork helmet. But that is in virtue of an equitable and logical principle, derived by them from
the high places of the new administration—
namely, that the Egypt of to-day belongs far
less to the Egyptians than to the noble foreigners
who have come to brandish there the torch of
civilisation.

In the evening, after dark, the really respectable travellers do not quit the brilliant dining
saloons of the hotels, and the quay is left quite
solitary beneath the stars. It is at such a time that
one is able to realise how extremely hospitable
certain of the natives are become. If, in an hour
of melancholy, you walk alone on the bank of
the Nile, smoking a cigarette, you will not fail to
be accosted by one of these good people, who,
misunderstanding the cause of the unrest in your
soul, offers eagerly, and with a touching frankness, to introduce you to the gayest of the young
ladies of the country.

In the other towns, which still remain purely
Egyptian, the people would never practise such
an excess of affability and good manners, which
have been learnt, beyond all question, from our
beneficent contact.

Assouan possesses also its little Oriental bazaar
—a little improvised, a little new perhaps; but
then one, at least, was needed, and that as quickly
as possible, in order that nothing might be wanting to the tourists.

The shopkeepers have contrived to provision
themselves (in the leading shops, under the
arcades of the Rue de Rivoli) with as much tact
as good taste, and the Cook ladies have the innocent illusion of making bargains every day.
One may even buy there, hung up by the tail,
stuffed with straw and looking extremely real,
the last crocodiles of Egypt, which, particularly
at the end of the season, may be had at very
advantageous prices.

Even the old Nile has allowed itself to be
fretted and brought up to date in the progress of
evolution.

First, the women, draped in black veils, who
come daily to draw the precious water, have for-
saken the fragile amphoræ of baked earth, which
had come to them from barbarous times—and
which the Orientalists grossly abused in their
pictures; and in their stead have taken to old tin
oil-cans, placed at their disposal by the kindness
of the big hotels. But they carry them in the
same easy graceful manner as erstwhile the discarded pottery, and without losing in the least
the gracious tanagrine outline.

And then there are the great tourist boats of the Agencies, which are here in abundance, for Assouan has the privilege of being the terminus of the line; and their whistlings, their revolving motors, their electric dynamos maintain from morning till night a captivating symphony. It might be urged perhaps against these structures that they resemble a little the washhouses on the Seine; but the Agencies, desirous of restoring to them a certain local colour, have given them names so notoriously Egyptian that one is reduced to silence. They are called Sesostris, Amenophis or Ramses the Great.

And finally there are the rowing boats, which carry passengers incessantly backwards and forwards between the river-banks. So long as the season remains at its height they are bedecked with a number of little flags of red cotton-cloth, or even of simple paper. The rowers, moreover, have been instructed to sing all the time the native songs which are accompanied by a derboucca player seated in the prow. Nay, they have even learnt to utter that rousing, stimulating cry which Anglo-Saxons use to express their enthusiasm or their joy: " Hip! hip! hurrah! " and you cannot conceive how well it sounds, coming between the Arab songs, which otherwise might be apt to grow monotonous.

.   .   .   .

But the triumph of Assouan is its desert. It begins at once without transition as soon as you pass the close-cropped turf of the last square. A desert which, except for the railroad and the telegraph poles, has all the charm of the real thing: the sand, the chaos of overthrown stones, the empty horizons—everything, in short, save the immensity and infinite solitude, the horror, in a word, which formerly made it so little desirable. It is a little astonishing, it must be owned, to find, on arriving there, that the rocks have been carefully numbered in white paint, and in some cases marked with a large cross " which catches the eye from a greater distance still " (*sic*). But I agree that the effect of the whole has lost nothing.

In the morning before the sun gets too hot, between breakfast and luncheon to be precise, all the good ladies in cork helmets and blue spectacles (dark-coloured spectacles are recommended on account of the glare) spread themselves over these solitudes, domesticated as it were to their use, with as much security as in Trafalgar Square or Kensington Gardens. Not seldom even you may see one of them making her way alone, book in hand, towards one of the picturesque rocks—No. 363, for example, or No. 364, if you like it better—which seems to be making signs to her with its white ticket, in a manner

which, to the uninitiated observer, might seem
even a little improper.

But what a sense of safety families may feel
here, to be sure! In spite of the huge numbers,
which at first sight look a little equivocal, nothing in the least degree reprehensible can happen
among these granites; which are, moreover, in
a single piece, without the least crack or hole
into which the straggler could contrive to crawl.
No. The figures and the crosses denote simply
blocks of stones, covered with hieroglyphics, and
correspond to a chaste catalogue where each
Pharaonic inscription may be found translated
in the most becoming language.

This ingenious ticketing of the stones of the
desert is due to the initiative of an English
Egyptologist.

THE PASSING
OF PHILÆ

CHAPTER XX

LEAVING Assouan—as soon as we have passed the last house—we come at once upon the desert. And now the night is falling, a cold February night, under a strange, copper-coloured sky.

Incontestably it is the desert, with its chaos of granite and sand, its warm tones and reddish colour. But there are telegraph poles and the lines of a railroad, which traverse it in company, and disappear in the empty horizon. And then too how paradoxical and ridiculous it seems to be travelling here on full security and in a carriage! (The most commonplace of hackney-carriages, which I hired by the hour on the quay of Assouan.) A desert indeed which preserves still its aspects of reality, but has become domesticated and tamed for the use of the tourists and the ladies.

First, immense cemeteries surrounded by sand at the beginning of these quasi-solitudes. Such old cemeteries of every epoch of history. The thousand little cupolas of saints of Islam are crumbling side by side with the Christian obelisks of the first centuries; and, underneath, the Pharaonic hypogea. In the twilight, all these ruins of the dead, all the scattered blocks of granite are mingled in mournful groupings, outlined in fantastic silhouette against the pale copper of the sky; broken arches, tilted domes, and rocks that rise up like tall phantoms.

Farther on, when we have left behind this region of tombs, the granites alone litter the expanse of sand, granites to which the usury of centuries has given the form of huge round beasts. In places they have been thrown one upon the other and make great heaps of monsters. Elsewhere they lie alone among the sands, as if lost in the midst of the infinitude of some dead sea-shore. The rails and the telegraph poles have disappeared; by the magic of the twilight everything is become grand again, beneath one of those evening skies of Egypt which, in winter, resemble cold cupolas of metal. And now it is that you feel yourself verily on the threshold of the profound desolations of Arabia, from which no barrier, after all, separates you. Were it not for the lack of verisimilitude in the carriage that has brought us hither, we should be able now to take this desert quite seriously—for in fact it has no limits.

After travelling for about three quarters of an hour, we see in the distance a number of lights, which have already been kindled in the growing darkness. They seem too bright to be those of an Arab encampment. And our driver turning round and pointing to them says: " Chelal! "

Chelal—that is the name of the Arab village, on the riverside, where you take the boat for Philæ. To our disgust the place is lighted by electricity. It consists of a station, a factory with a long smoking chimney, and a dozen or so suspicious-looking taverns, reeking of alcohol, without which, it would seem, our European civilisation could not implant itself in a new country.

And here we embark for Philæ. A number of boats are ready: for the tourists allured by many advertisements flock hither every winter in docile herds. All the boats, without a single exception, are profusely decorated with little English flags, as if for some regatta on the Thames. There is no escape therefore from this beflagging of a foreign holiday—and we set out with a homesick song of Nubia, which the boatmen sing to the cadence of the oars.

The copper-coloured heaven remains so impregnated with cold light that we still see clearly. We are amid magnificent tragic scenery on a lake surrounded by a kind of fearful amphitheatre outlined on all sides by the mountains of the desert. It was at the bottom of this granite circus that the Nile used to flow, forming fresh islets, on which the eternal verdure of the palm-

trees contrasted with the high desolate mountains
that surrounded it like a wall. To-day, on account of the barrage established by the English,
the water has steadily risen, like a tide that will
never recede; and this lake, almost a little sea,
replaces the meanderings of the river and has
succeeded in submerging the sacred islets. The
sanctuary of Isis—which was enthroned for thousands of years on the summit of a hill, crowded
with temples and colonnades and statues—still
half emerges; but it is alone and will soon go the
way of the others. There it is, beyond, like a
great rock, at this hour in which the night begins
to obscure everything.

Nowhere but in Upper Egypt have the winter
nights these transparencies of absolute emptiness
nor these sinister colourings. As the light gradually fails, the sky passes from copper to
bronze, but remains always metallic. The zenith
becomes brownish like a brazen shield, while the
setting sun alone retains its yellow colour, growing slowly paler till it is almost of the whiteness
of latten; and, above, the mountains of the desert
edge their sharp outlines with a tint of burnt
sienna. To-night a freezing wind blows fiercely
in our faces. To the continual chant of the
rowers we pass slowly over the artificial lake,
which is upheld as it were in the air by the
English masonry, invisible now in the distance,

but divined nevertheless and revolting. A sac-
rilegious lake one might call it, since it hides
beneath its troubled waters ruins beyond all
price; temples of the gods of Egypt, churches
of the first centuries of Christianity, obelisks,
inscriptions and emblems. It is over these things
that we now pass, while the spray splashes in
our faces, and the foam of a thousand angry little billows.

We draw near to what was once the holy isle.
In places dying palm-trees, whose long trunks are
to-day under water, still show their moistened
plumes and give an appearance of inundation,
almost of cataclysm.

Before coming to the sanctuary of Isis, we
touch at the kiosk of Philæ, which has been
reproduced in the pictures of every age, and is
as celebrated even as the Sphinx and the pyramids. It used to stand on a pedestal of high
rocks, and around it the date-trees swayed their
bouquets of aerial palms. To-day it has no
longer a base; its columns rise separately from
this kind of suspended lake. It looks as if it
had been constructed in the water for the purpose
of some royal naumachy. We enter with our
boat — a strange port indeed, in its ancient
grandeur; a port of a nameless melancholy, particularly at this yellow hour of the closing twilight, and under these icy winds that come to

us mercilessly from the neighbouring deserts.
And yet how adorable it is, this kiosk of Philæ,
in this the abandonment that precedes its downfall! Its columns placed, as it were, upon something unstable, become thereby more slender,
seem to raise higher still the stone foliage of
their capitals. A veritable kiosk of dreamland
now, which one feels is about to disappear for
ever under these waters which will subside no
more!

And now, for another few moments, it grows
quite light again, and tints of a warmer copper
reappear in the sky. Often in Egypt when the
sun has set and you think the light is gone, this
furtive recoloration of the air comes thus to surprise you, before the darkness finally descends.
The reddish tints seem to return to the slender
shafts that surround us, and also, beyond, to the
temple of the goddess, standing there like a sheer
rock in the middle of this little sea, which the
wind covers with foam.

On leaving the kiosk our boat—on this deep
usurping water, among the submerged palm-trees
—makes a detour in order to lead us to the temple
by the road which the pilgrims of olden times
used to travel on foot—by that way which, a little
while ago, was still magnificent, bordered with
colonnades and statues. But now the road is
entirely submerged, and will never be seen again.

Between its double row of columns the water lifts
us to the height of the capitals, which alone
emerge and which we could touch with our hands.
It seems like some journey of the end of time, in
a kind of deserted Venice, which is about to topple
over, to sink and be forgotten.

We arrive at the temple. Above our heads
rise the enormous pylons, ornamented with figures in bas-relief: an Isis who stretches out her
arms as if she were making signs to us, and numerous other divinities gesticulating mysteriously.
The door which opens in the thickness of these
walls is low, besides being half flooded, and
gives on to depths already in darkness. We
row on and enter the sanctuary, and as soon as
our boat has crossed the sacred threshold the
boatmen stop their song and suddenly give voice
to the new cry that has been taught them for the
benefit of the tourists: " Hip! hip! hip! hurrah! " Coming at this moment, when, with
heart oppressed by all the utilitarian vandalism
that surrounds us, we were entering the sanctuary, what an effect of gross and imbecile profanation this bellowing of English joy produces!
The boatmen know, moreover, that they have
been displaced, that their day has gone for ever;
perhaps even, in the depths of their Nubian souls,
they understand us, for all that we have imposed
silence on them. The darkness increases within,

although the place is open to the sky, and the icy wind blows more mournfully than it did outside. A penetrating humidity—a humidity altogether unknown in this country before the inundation—chills us to the bone. We are now in that part of the temple which was left uncovered, the part where the faithful used to kneel. The sonority of the granites round about exaggerates the noise of the oars on the enclosed water, and there is something confusing in the thought that we are rowing and floating between the walls where formerly, and for centuries, men were used to prostrate themselves with their foreheads on the stones.

And now it is quite dark; the hour grows late. We have to bring the boat close to the walls to distinguish the hieroglyphs and rigid gods which are engraved there as finely as by the burin. These walls, washed for nearly four years by the inundation, have already taken on at the base that sad blackish colour which may be seen on the old Venetian palaces.

Halt and silence. It is dark and cold. The oars no longer move, and we hear only the sighing of the wind and the lapping of the water against the columns and the bas-reliefs—and then suddenly there comes the noise of a heavy body falling, followed by endless eddies. A great carved stone has plunged, at its due hour, to rejoin in the black chaos below its fellows that have already disappeared, to rejoin the sub-merged temples and old Coptic churches, and the town of the first Christian centuries—all that was once the Isle of Philæ, the " pearl of Egypt," one of the marvels of the world.

The darkness is now extreme and we can see no longer. Let us go and shelter, no matter where, to await the moon. At the end of this uncovered hall there opens a door which gives on to deep night. It is the holy of holies, heavily roofed with granite, the highest part of the temple, the only part which the waters have not yet reached, and there we are able to put foot to earth. Our footsteps resound noisily on the large resonant flags, and the owls take to flight. Pro-found darkness; the wind and the dampness freeze us. Three hours to go before the rising of the moon; to wait in this place would be our death. Rather let us return to Chelal, and shelter our-selves in any lodging that offers, however wretched it may be.

.   .   .   .

A tavern of the horrible village in the light of an electric lamp. It reeks of absinthe, this desert tavern, in which we warm ourselves at a little smoking fire. It has been hastily built of old tin boxes, of the debris of whisky cases, and by way of mural decoration the landlord, an

ignorant Maltese, has pasted everywhere pictures
cut from our European pornographic news-
papers. During our hours of waiting, Nubians
and Arabians follow one another hither, asking
for drink, and are supplied with brimming glass-
fuls of our alcoholic beverages. They are the
workers in the new factories who were formerly
healthy beings, living in the open air. But now
their faces are stained with coal dust, and their
haggard eyes look unhappy and ill.

.   .   .   .

The rising of the moon is fortunately at hand.
Once more in our boat we make our way slowly
towards the sad rock which to-day is Philæ.
The wind has fallen with the night, as happens
almost invariably in this country in winter, and
the lake is calm. To the mournful yellow sky
has succeeded one that is blue-black, infinitely
distant, where the stars of Egypt scintillate in
myriads.

A great glimmering light shows now in the
east and at length the full moon rises, not blood-
coloured as in our climates but straightway very
luminous, and surrounded by an aureole of a kind
of mist, caused by the eternal dust of the sands.
And when we return to the baseless kiosk—lulled
always by the Nubian song of the boatmen
—a great disc is already illuminating everything
with a gentle splendour. As our little boat winds

in and out, we see the great ruddy disc passing and repassing between the high columns, so
striking in their archaism, whose images are
repeated in the water, that is now grown calm—
more than ever a kiosk of dreamland, a kiosk of
old-world magic.

In returning to the temple of the goddess, we
follow for a second time the submerged road between the capitals and friezes of the colonnade
which emerge like a row of little reefs.

In the uncovered hall which forms the entrance
to the temple, it is still dark between the sovereign
granites. Let us moor our boat against one of
the walls and await the good pleasure of the
moon. As soon as she shall have risen high
enough to cast her light here, we shall see
clearly.

It begins by a rosy glimmer on the summit
of the pylons; and then takes the form of a
luminous triangle, very clearly defined, which
grows gradually larger on the immense wall.
Little by little it descends towards the base of
the temple, revealing to us by degrees the intimidating presence of the bas-reliefs, the gods,
goddesses and hieroglyphs, and the assemblies
of people who make signs among themselves.
We are no longer alone—a whole world of
phantoms has been evoked around us by the
moon, some little, some very large. They had

been hiding there in the shadow and now suddenly they recommence their mute conversations, without breaking the profound silence,
using only their expressive hands and raised
fingers. And now also the colossal Isis begins
to appear—the one carved on the left of the
portico by which you enter; first, her refined
head with its bird's helmet, surmounted by a
solar disc; then, as the light continues to
descend, her neck and shoulders, and her arm,
raised to make who knows what mysterious,
indicating sign; and finally the slim nudity of
her torso, and her hips close bound in a sheath.
Behold her now, the goddess, come completely
out of the shadow. . . . But she seems surprised
and disturbed at seeing at her feet, instead of the
stones she had known for two thousand years, her
own likeness, a reflection of herself, that stretches
away, reversed in the mirror of the water. . . .

And suddenly, in the midst of the deep nocturnal calm of this temple, isolated here in the
lake, comes again the sound of a kind of mournful booming, of things that topple, precious
stones that become detached and fall—and then,
on the surface of the lake, a thousand concentric
circles form, chase one another and disappear,
ruffling indefinitely this mirror embanked between
the terrible granites, in which Isis regards herself
sorrowfully.

Postscript.—The submerging of Philæ, as we know, has increased by no less than seventy-five millions of pounds the annual yield of the surrounding land. Encouraged by this success, the English propose next year to raise the barrage of the Nile another twenty feet. As a consequence this sanctuary of Isis will be completely submerged, the greater part of the ancient temples of Nubia will be under water, and fever will infect the country. But, on the other hand, the cultivation of cotton will be enormously facilitated. . . .

Index

305

Index